Introduction: Embark on Your Entrepreneurial Odyssey

In the bustling world of startups, where dreams are woven into code, innovation is currency, and resilience is the heartbeat of success, comes a guiding light forged from the crucible of experience. Welcome to the transformative journey outlined in "From Dream to Nightmare: 108 Mistakes That Can Sink Your Startup" an illuminating chronicle authored by the seasoned entrepreneur, Arpal Jain.

As the founder of a groundbreaking B2B e-commerce startup, Arpal Jain embarked on a voyage that mirrored the aspirations and challenges faced by countless entrepreneurs. His story is one of audacious dreams, tireless nights, and the unwavering pursuit of excellence. Like many visionaries, Arpal found himself navigating stormy seas, encountering uncharted territories, and grappling with the complexities inherent in birthing and nurturing a startup.

MEET ARPAL JAIN: ARCHITECT OF INNOVATION

Arpal Jain is not just an author; he is a fellow traveler on the entrepreneurial odyssey—a journey marked by the highs of success and the lows of formidable challenges. His B2B e-commerce startup, born from a spark of inspiration, faced its share of tribulations. Arpal, however, did not merely weather the storm; he transformed setbacks into stepping stones for growth.

In the crucible of his startup journey, Arpal encountered the maze of mistakes that can ensnare even the most visionary minds. The journey was fraught with missteps, unexpected hurdles, and the daunting task of learning from experiences that often felt like harsh tutors. Yet, within each mistake, Arpal found the seeds of wisdom that germinated into this invaluable guide for every entrepreneur setting sail on their startup voyage.

Why This Book Matters: A Beacon for Every Entrepreneur

"From Dream to Nightmare: 108 Mistakes That Can Sink Your Startup" is more than a book; it's an entrepreneur's survival guide penned by seasoned innovator Arpal Jain. It's a beacon in the storm, offering a candid narrative of entrepreneurship—one marked by resilience, adaptability, and the invaluable wisdom that arises from overcoming challenges.

Arpal's insights, forged in the crucible of his B2B e-commerce startup, resonate as a relatable and indispensable roadmap for every business trailblazer. This book isn't just a read; it's a mentor, a compass, and a source of inspiration, urging entrepreneurs to view mistakes not as setbacks but as essential milestones on the path to success.

WHAT TO EXPECT: WISDOM IN EVERY PAGE

Within the pages of this book, Arpal Jain shares not only his own trials and triumphs but also the distilled wisdom gained from overcoming pitfalls that plague startups. From the intricacies of financial management to the nuances of team dynamics, Arpal's insights provide a roadmap for steering through the challenges that define the startup landscape.

Arpal's compelling narrative invites you, the reader, to embark on your entrepreneurial odyssey equipped with the knowledge garnered from real-world experiences. Each chapter resonates with the heartbeat of an entrepreneur who has faced adversity head-on and emerged with the battle scars of a seasoned innovator.

Welcome Aboard: Your Entrepreneurial Journey Begins Here

As you delve into "From Dream to Nightmare: 108 Mistakes That Can Sink Your Startup" consider Arpal Jain not just as an author but as your mentor, guiding you through the intricate dance of entrepreneurship. The mistakes outlined within these pages are not roadblocks but stepping stones, opportunities for growth, and catalysts for transformation.

Whether you are a seasoned entrepreneur or a budding visionary, Arpal's insights will resonate with you, offering a compass for navigating the unpredictable seas of startup life. So, welcome aboard. Your entrepreneurial journey begins here, guided by the wisdom of an entrepreneur who has ventured where you are about to tread.

May this book be your companion, your guide, and your source of inspiration as you embark on your entrepreneurial odyssey.

"From Dream to Nightmare: 108 Mistakes That Can Sink Your Startup"

IGNORING MARKET RESEARCH

Chapter 1: The Illusion of a Brilliant Idea

Once upon a time in the bustling city of Innovaria, two ambitious friends, Alex and Taylor, decided to turn their passion for sustainable living into a groundbreaking startup. They were convinced that their idea for solar-powered, self-sustaining homes would revolutionize the housing industry. Eager to make their dream a reality, they dove headfirst into the business without conducting proper market research.

As they developed their prototype and poured their savings into the project, they were blissfully unaware of a growing trend in the market—smart, eco-friendly apartments were already gaining traction, and there was a considerable lack of interest in single-family, off-grid homes.

Impact:

Ignoring market research proved to be their Achilles' heel. The duo discovered that potential customers were more interested in affordable, community-centric living than standalone, high-cost eco-homes. The market was already saturated with alternative solutions, and they had failed to identify the changing preferences of their target audience.

Facing a harsh reality, Alex and Taylor struggled to pivot their concept, wasting precious time and resources. Their dream of a revolutionary housing solution turned into a financial nightmare. The lesson learned was clear: never underestimate the importance of market research —it's the compass that guides your startup through the turbulent seas of business.

Underestimating the Power of a Strong Team

Chapter 2: The Lone Wolf's Gambit

In the heart of Innovaria, a tech prodigy named Chris was determined to develop a cutting-edge app that would revolutionize personal finance management. Driven by a fierce sense of independence, Chris believed they could handle all aspects of the startup alone, from coding to marketing. The thought of sharing the spotlight with a team seemed unnecessary and burdensome.

As the app gained traction, Chris found it increasingly challenging to manage the workload. Balancing development, customer support, and marketing efforts became an overwhelming task. The initial excitement of going solo turned into burnout, and the quality of the product suffered.

Impact:

Chris's reluctance to build a team had a cascading effect on the startup. The lack of diverse perspectives led to blind spots in the product's design, and customer feedback was often overlooked. As the workload intensified, the app's development slowed down, causing frustration among users and damaging the startup's reputation.

Realizing the need for a collaborative effort, Chris belatedly started assembling a team. However, the damage was done—the app's initial momentum had waned, and potential investors were skeptical about the founder's ability to lead a team effectively.

The lesson was clear: underestimating the power of a strong, collaborative team can cripple even the most promising startups. Success is seldom a solo journey, and recognizing the strengths of others is key to navigating the complex landscape of entrepreneurship.

Neglecting the Importance of Financial Planning:

Chapter 3: The Mirage of Infinite Funding

In a vibrant corner of Innovaria, Sarah, a charismatic entrepreneur, was on a mission to disrupt the fitness industry with a state-of-the-art virtual reality workout platform. Armed with a compelling vision and a persuasive pitch, Sarah secured a substantial amount of seed funding from enthusiastic investors. Excitement was in the air as the team poured their energy into developing the product.

However, amidst the creative fervor, financial planning took a back seat. The initial investment was treated as an endless pool of resources, and the team operated with the assumption that more funding would magically appear when needed.

Impact:

As development progressed, unforeseen challenges arose. The team encountered technical setbacks and underestimated the costs of marketing and user acquisition. The initial influx of capital dwindled faster than expected, leaving the startup in a precarious financial position.

With no contingency plan in place, Sarah found herself in a race against time to secure additional funding. Investors, initially drawn by the vision, were hesitant to inject more money without evidence of a sound financial strategy. The startup's once-promising trajectory began to stall, and the pressure mounted.

The lesson learned was harsh but invaluable: neglecting financial planning is a perilous gamble. Even with a groundbreaking idea, a lack of fiscal responsibility can transform a promising startup into a cautionary tale. In the unpredictable world of entrepreneurship, a well-thought-out financial roadmap is the compass that guides a startup toward sustainability.

OVERLOOKING THE SIGNIFICANCE OF MARKETING AND BRANDING

Chapter 4: The Invisible Marvel

In the bustling city of Innovaria, a team of tech enthusiasts led by Olivia was developing a revolutionary gadget that promised to redefine communication. The product was brilliant, the technology cutting-edge, but Olivia believed that the innovation alone would speak volumes. With a limited budget, marketing and branding took a backseat as the team focused solely on product development.

As the launch date approached, excitement turned into bewilderment. The groundbreaking gadget, despite its marvels, remained largely unnoticed in the market. Olivia had neglected the crucial aspects of marketing and branding, assuming that the product's brilliance would automatically attract attention.

Impact:

The innovative gadget, lost in the sea of competitors, struggled to make its mark. Potential users were unaware of its existence, and the startup's outreach efforts fell flat. Olivia soon realized that a lack of effective marketing and branding had rendered their technological marvel invisible in the crowded marketplace.

Frantically trying to salvage the situation, the team had to allocate emergency funds for a last-minute marketing campaign. The delayed efforts, however, failed to generate the desired buzz, and the product launch fell short of expectations.

The lesson learned was clear: in a world inundated with innovations, the success of a startup isn't solely determined by the quality of the product. Ignoring the significance of marketing and branding is akin to building a masterpiece in the dark—a futile endeavor that diminishes the potential impact of even the most brilliant ideas.

Ignoring the Customer Feedback Loop

Chapter 5: The Deaf Ears of Innovation

In the heart of Innovaria, a dynamic duo, Maya and Ryan, were on a mission to revolutionize the food delivery industry with their innovative meal planning app. Fueled by their passion for healthy living, they meticulously designed the app, confident that they knew exactly what their users needed.

As the app launched, Maya and Ryan were flooded with user feedback. However, convinced of their own insights, they dismissed much of it as minor complaints, believing that the brilliance of their concept would overshadow any initial hiccups.

Impact:

Over time, the app struggled to gain traction. Negative reviews piled up, and users started abandoning the platform. Unbeknownst to Maya and Ryan, their initial user base held valuable insights that, if heeded, could have steered the startup towards success.

By ignoring the customer feedback loop, Maya and Ryan failed to address critical issues with the app's user interface and overall user experience. Competitors, attuned to their users' needs, swiftly captured the market share that Maya and Ryan had initially overlooked.

The harsh reality hit them: innovation isn't a solo journey. Success hinges on understanding and incorporating user feedback into the iterative process. The failure to establish a robust feedback loop meant their innovative solution fell short of meeting the real needs of their target audience.

Neglecting Scalability in Product Development

Chapter 6: The Mirage of Endless Growth

In a corner of Innovaria, a team led by Mark embarked on a journey to disrupt the e-commerce space with a unique online marketplace for handmade crafts. The initial response was overwhelming, and orders poured in. Excitement filled the air as Mark and his team worked tirelessly to fulfill requests and maintain the high quality that set their platform apart.

However, in the race to meet immediate demand, they neglected to consider the long-term scalability of their operations. The artisanal crafts, once made with care and attention, began to suffer in quality. The infrastructure couldn't handle the influx of orders, and customer satisfaction plummeted.

Impact:

As word spread about the declining quality and delayed deliveries, the startup's reputation crumbled. Negative reviews flooded in, and loyal customers turned away. Mark and his team found themselves caught in a vicious cycle—increased demand led to compromised quality, resulting in customer dissatisfaction, which further damaged the brand.

Realizing the need for scalability, Mark attempted to restructure operations. However, the damage had been done, and competitors had seized the opportunity to fill the gap in the market. The once-thriving startup became a cautionary tale of the importance of scalability in product development.

The lesson learned was profound: while rapid growth is exciting, neglecting to build a scalable infrastructure can jeopardize the very foundation of a startup. Success isn't just about meeting current demand; it's about laying the groundwork for sustainable growth without compromising on quality.

Disregarding the Importance of a Strong Company Culture

Chapter 7: The Fractured Team

Nestled in the heart of Innovaria, a startup led by Emma and James set out to revolutionize remote work with a groundbreaking project management tool. Excitement filled the air as the team worked tirelessly to bring their vision to life. In the midst of deadlines and deliverables, the founders overlooked the crucial element of cultivating a strong company culture.

As the pressure mounted, communication within the team began to break down. The initial camaraderie was replaced by a sense of isolation, and employees felt disconnected from the company's mission. The founders, engrossed in the day-to-day operations, failed to recognize the subtle signs of a crumbling company culture.

Impact:

Morale within the startup hit an all-time low. Employee turnover skyrocketed, and the remaining team members struggled to maintain productivity. The initial synergy that fueled creativity and innovation gave way to a toxic work environment. The startup's reputation as an exciting place to work eroded, making it challenging to attract top talent.

Realizing the consequences of neglecting company culture, Emma and James attempted to foster a positive work environment. However, the damage was extensive, and rebuilding trust proved to be an uphill battle. The founders learned the hard way that a strong company culture isn't just a buzzword —it's the glue that holds a startup together in times of challenge and triumph.

The lesson was clear: success isn't just about the product; it's about the people behind it. A neglected company culture can unravel even the most innovative startups, emphasizing the importance of fostering a workplace where creativity and collaboration thrive.

Underestimating Regulatory Compliance

Chapter 8: The Legal Quagmire

In a bustling corner of Innovaria, a group of entrepreneurs led by Carla set out to disrupt the healthcare industry with a revolutionary telemedicine platform. Excitement fueled their ambitions, and the team poured their energy into developing a user-friendly and accessible solution. However, in their zeal for innovation, they underestimated the complexities of regulatory compliance in the healthcare sector.

Unaware of the intricate legal landscape governing telemedicine, Carla and her team launched their platform without fully understanding the necessary compliance requirements. As the platform gained traction, regulatory authorities took notice, and the startup found itself entangled in a legal quagmire.

Impact:

The regulatory hurdles proved to be more than just a minor inconvenience. Fines and legal fees began to accumulate, draining the startup's resources. The platform faced temporary shutdowns, causing panic among users and damaging the company's reputation. Investors, initially drawn by the platform's potential, grew wary as the legal battles unfolded.

In a desperate attempt to navigate the regulatory maze, Carla and her team had to divert valuable time and resources away from product development. The dream of revolutionizing telemedicine became a nightmare of legal woes and financial strain.

The lesson was stark: underestimating regulatory compliance can be a fatal mistake for startups, particularly in highly regulated industries. Success isn't just about innovation; it's about understanding and adhering to the legal frameworks that govern the business landscape.

Failing to Adapt to Technological Changes

Chapter 9: The Dinosaur's Dilemma

In the heart of Innovaria, a seasoned entrepreneur named Michael was at the helm of a successful e-commerce platform that had dominated the market for years. Confident in the platform's stability, Michael and his team became complacent, failing to stay abreast of emerging technologies and industry trends.

As the winds of change swept through the digital landscape, new, more agile competitors emerged with innovative features and superior user experiences. Michael's e-commerce platform, once considered cutting-edge, began to feel outdated and clunky in comparison.

Impact:

Customers, once loyal to the platform, started migrating to competitors offering a more seamless and modern experience. Michael, initially dismissive of these changes, soon found his market share dwindling. The failure to adapt to technological shifts left the once-thriving platform struggling to retain relevance.

Realizing the gravity of the situation, Michael attempted to implement updates and improvements, but the damage was already done. The startup, once a giant in the industry, faced an uphill battle to regain its competitive edge. The reluctance to embrace technological changes had transformed a market leader into a digital dinosaur on the brink of extinction.

The lesson was crystal clear: in the rapidly evolving landscape of technology, failing to adapt is akin to signing a startup's death warrant. Innovation isn't a one-time effort; it's a continuous journey of evolution and adaptation to emerging technologies and market trends.

Overlooking the Importance of Diversity and Inclusion

Chapter 10: The Echo Chamber Effect

In a vibrant corner of Innovaria, a group of entrepreneurs led by Jasmine set out to create a social networking platform designed to foster meaningful connections among users. Excitement filled the air as the team brainstormed ideas and worked diligently to bring their vision to life. However, in the midst of their creative fervor, they inadvertently overlooked the importance of building a diverse and inclusive team.

The startup team, while passionate, shared similar backgrounds and perspectives. Unintentionally, they created an echo chamber, where ideas went unchallenged, and potential blind spots in their product were left unaddressed. The consequences of this oversight became apparent as the platform launched.

Impact:

While the platform resonated with some users, it failed to connect with a broader audience. The oversight in diversity and inclusion became evident in the platform's features, which didn't cater to the needs and preferences of a more diverse user base. Competitors, with a more inclusive approach, quickly gained traction, leaving Jasmine's startup struggling to expand its user demographics.

Recognizing the need for diversity and inclusion, Jasmine tried to course-correct by diversifying the team and incorporating feedback from a wider range of perspectives. However, the initial misstep had already hindered the platform's growth, and users who felt excluded in the early stages were hesitant to return.

The lesson was poignant: a lack of diversity and inclusion can stifle innovation and limit a startup's ability to resonate with a diverse user base. Success in the modern business landscape requires a commitment to building a team that reflects the diversity of the broader community and understanding the varied needs of different user groups.

Overestimating the Initial Hype and Underestimating Long-Term Execution

Chapter 11: The Fading Spark

In the heart of Innovaria, a group of young entrepreneurs led by Alex embarked on a mission to disrupt the entertainment industry with a unique streaming platform. Fueled by a groundbreaking concept, they generated significant buzz during the pre-launch phase. The excitement reached a fever pitch as the platform finally went live, drawing attention from users and media alike.

However, intoxicated by the initial hype, the team failed to recognize that sustained success required more than just a splashy launch. As the novelty wore off, user engagement plateaued, and the competition intensified. The startup found itself grappling with the reality that maintaining momentum required relentless dedication to long-term execution.

IMPACT:

The initial surge of users proved to be short-lived, and the startup struggled to retain its audience. The lack of a robust long-term strategy led to a decline in content quality, technical issues, and a failure to adapt to changing user preferences. The once-promising platform lost its appeal, and users flocked to more established competitors.

Realizing the importance of sustained effort, Alex and the team attempted to reinvigorate the platform. However, the initial burst of hype had dissipated, and rebuilding trust among users proved to be a formidable challenge. The startup became a cautionary tale of overestimating the power of initial excitement while underestimating the ongoing commitment required for success.

The lesson learned was profound: while a strong launch can create momentum, the real test of a startup's viability lies in its ability to execute consistently over the long term. Success is not a sprint but a marathon that demands continuous innovation, adaptation, and a steadfast commitment to delivering value to users.

OVERLOOKING THE IMPORTANCE OF CYBERSECURITY

Chapter 12: The Breach That Shattered Trust

In the heart of Innovaria, a team led by Danielle was on a mission to create a secure and user-friendly password management app. Recognizing the increasing importance of cybersecurity, they poured their energy into developing a solution that promised to keep users' sensitive information safe. However, in their pursuit of creating a seamless user experience, they inadvertently overlooked the critical aspect of cybersecurity.

As the app gained popularity, hackers took notice. Exploiting vulnerabilities that the team had failed to address, a cyberattack compromised the security of the platform. User data, once considered secure, was now in the hands of malicious actors.

Impact:

The fallout was swift and severe. Users lost trust in the app, and the startup faced a wave of negative publicity. Attempts to reassure users and patch security flaws were too little, too late. The damage to the startup's reputation was irreparable, and users migrated to competitors offering more robust security measures.

The financial toll was significant as well. Legal battles, fines, and the cost of rebuilding the platform's security infrastructure strained the startup's resources. The oversight in cybersecurity not only jeopardized user trust but also threatened the very existence of the once-promising app.

The lesson learned was harsh but crucial: in the digital age, overlooking cybersecurity is a recipe for disaster. The trust of users is hard-earned and easily shattered by security breaches. Prioritizing cybersecurity from the outset is not just a precautionary measure; it's a fundamental responsibility that can safeguard a startup's reputation and viability.

IGNORING THE POWER OF NETWORKING AND INDUSTRY RELATIONSHIPS

Chapter 13: The Isolated Island

In a dynamic corner of Innovaria, a team led by Marcus set out to revolutionize the gaming industry with an innovative virtual reality gaming experience. The initial development stages were exhilarating, and the team poured their creativity into crafting a unique product. However, amidst the excitement, Marcus and his team inadvertently became isolated, working in a silo without actively engaging with the broader gaming industry.

As the launch date approached, Marcus realized the strategic error in neglecting to build meaningful industry relationships. The startup lacked visibility, and potential partnerships that could have amplified their reach remained untapped. The failure to network effectively left the team stranded on an isolated island, disconnected from valuable opportunities and industry insights.

Impact:

The consequences became evident post-launch. While the product was innovative, it struggled to gain widespread attention. Competitors with strong industry relationships secured collaborations, sponsorships, and media coverage that propelled them ahead. Marcus found himself playing catch-up in an industry where relationships and networking were paramount.

Realizing the missed opportunities, Marcus attempted to forge connections post-launch. However, rebuilding relationships proved to be a gradual process, and the initial momentum had already been lost. The startup learned that success in the gaming industry, like many others, isn't just about a great product—it's about navigating the intricate web of industry relationships.

The lesson learned was clear: networking isn't just a luxury; it's a strategic necessity. Building relationships within the industry opens doors to collaborations, mentorship, and valuable insights that can propel a startup forward.

Underestimating the Impact of Economic Trends

Chapter 14: Riding the Unstable Wave

In the economic hub of Innovaria, a team led by Emily set out to create a financial planning app that would empower users to navigate the complexities of personal finance. The initial stages were marked by optimism, but as the app neared completion, an unforeseen economic downturn swept across the region.

Blindsided by the sudden shift in economic trends, Emily's team faced challenges they hadn't anticipated. The app, designed for a stable financial landscape, struggled to adapt to the economic uncertainties that affected user behaviors and financial priorities.

Impact:

The economic downturn resulted in a decline in user engagement and a shift in consumer spending habits. Users, grappling with financial uncertainties, sought different solutions than what Emily's app initially addressed. The startup faced increased churn, and attracting new users in an economically strained environment became a formidable challenge.

Realizing the need for adaptability, Emily and her team attempted to pivot the app's features to align with changing economic realities. However, the damage had been done, and the initial setback proved difficult to overcome. The startup learned that economic trends could significantly impact user adoption, making it crucial for businesses to incorporate flexibility and foresight into their strategies.

The lesson was profound: economic stability isn't guaranteed, and startups must be prepared to navigate turbulent economic waters. Understanding the broader economic landscape and designing products or services with adaptability in mind is essential for long-term sustainability.

LACKING A CLEAR EXIT STRATEGY

Chapter 15: The Road to Nowhere

In a strategic corner of Innovaria, a group of entrepreneurs led by Olivia set out to create a revolutionary augmented reality platform. Fueled by passion and ambition, they poured their resources into developing groundbreaking technology. However, in the midst of their creative journey, they neglected to establish a clear exit strategy.

As the startup gained traction, investors and stakeholders began inquiring about the long-term vision and potential exit opportunities. Olivia, caught up in the day-to-day challenges of scaling the business, had not given due consideration to the importance of having a well-defined exit strategy.

Impact:

The absence of a clear exit plan left stakeholders in limbo. Uncertainty loomed over the startup's future, and potential investors were hesitant to commit without a transparent roadmap for potential exits. The lack of strategic planning hindered the startup's ability to secure additional funding and form partnerships that could have accelerated its growth.

Realizing the oversight, Olivia attempted to craft an exit strategy on the fly. However, the hasty approach lacked the precision and foresight needed to inspire confidence among stakeholders. The startup found itself at a crossroads, with no clear direction for the future.

The lesson was stark: the journey of a startup should include not just the thrill of creation but also a thoughtful consideration of the endgame. Whether through acquisition, merger, or initial public offering (IPO), having a well-articulated exit strategy is crucial for aligning stakeholder interests, attracting investment, and navigating the complex landscape of business evolution.

Neglecting the Importance of Continuous Learning and Adaptation

Chapter 16: The Stagnant Pool

In a dynamic corner of Innovaria, a team led by Carlos embarked on a mission to create an artificial intelligence-driven analytics platform. The initial stages were marked by rapid innovation, and the team celebrated early successes. However, as they basked in their achievements, they unknowingly entered a dangerous territory—complacency.

Neglecting the importance of continuous learning and adaptation, the team failed to stay abreast of evolving technologies and industry trends. The once-cutting-edge platform began to lose its competitive edge, and competitors leveraging the latest advancements started to outpace Carlos's startup.

Impact:

The consequences of stagnation were severe. Users, initially drawn by the platform's innovation, migrated to competitors offering more advanced features. The startup's reputation suffered, and potential investors questioned its ability to remain relevant in a rapidly evolving landscape.

Recognizing the need for adaptation, Carlos and his team attempted to catch up by integrating new technologies. However, the time lost and the perception of falling behind proved challenging to overcome. The startup learned that success in the fast-paced world of technology requires a commitment to continuous learning and adaptation.

The lesson was clear: the journey of innovation is ongoing, and startups must embrace a culture of continuous learning to stay ahead of the curve. Failing to adapt to technological advancements and industry shifts can turn a once-promising startup into a stagnant pool, devoid of the vitality needed for sustained success.

Overextending Resources Without a Clear ROI

Chapter 17: The Burnout Spiral

In a high-energy corner of Innovaria, a group of entrepreneurs led by Tony set out to disrupt the fitness industry with a comprehensive health and wellness app. Fueled by passion and determination, they poured significant resources into developing features and partnerships, with the belief that a comprehensive offering would guarantee success.

However, in the pursuit of an all-encompassing solution, Tony's team overextended their resources without a clear focus on return on investment (ROI). The app became a feature-rich behemoth, but the true impact on user engagement and revenue remained unclear.

IMPACT:

The consequences of overextension were twofold. First, the team faced burnout as they tried to manage the complexity of a multifaceted platform. Second, the lack of a clear ROI made it challenging to attract investors and partners who were skeptical about the sustainability of the startup's expansive approach.

Realizing the need for a strategic focus, Tony and his team attempted to streamline the app's features and highlight key value propositions. However, the initial overextension had strained resources and tarnished the startup's reputation for being focused and efficient.

The lesson learned was profound: while ambition is admirable, overextending resources without a clear ROI can lead to burnout, diminished product quality, and skepticism from stakeholders. Success lies not just in offering a multitude of features but in delivering meaningful value that aligns with the priorities of users and investors.

Underestimating the Importance of Resilience in Entrepreneurship

Chapter 18: The Uncharted Storm

In a resilient corner of Innovaria, a team led by Maya set out to create a weather prediction platform using advanced machine learning algorithms. The startup faced early challenges, but Maya's unwavering determination and resilience carried the team through turbulent times.

However, as the startup gained traction, Maya underestimated the toll that the unpredictable nature of entrepreneurship could take on her team's resilience. The initial setbacks were mere ripples compared to the uncharted storm that awaited them.

Impact:

As the startup encountered unforeseen challenges—market fluctuations, technical hurdles, and unexpected competition—the team's morale wavered. Maya, caught off guard, struggled to maintain the same level of resilience that had fueled the startup's early successes. The team's collective spirit faltered, and the startup faced a crisis of confidence.

Realizing the importance of resilience, Maya attempted to rally her team and instill a renewed sense of determination. However, the initial blow had taken its toll, and rebuilding resilience proved to be a gradual process. The startup learned that resilience isn't just a personal trait; it's a collective strength that must be nurtured and reinforced during both calm and stormy seas.

The lesson was clear: entrepreneurship is a journey fraught with uncertainties, and underestimating the importance of resilience can leave a startup vulnerable to the challenges that lie ahead. Building a culture of resilience ensures that a team can weather the storms and emerge stronger on the other side.

Ignoring the Impact of Global Events on Business Operations

Chapter 19: The Global Wake-Up Call

In the interconnected world of Innovaria, a team led by Elena set out to create an international e-commerce platform. The startup thrived in a global marketplace, connecting buyers and sellers from different corners of the world. However, the team failed to anticipate the potential impact of unforeseen global events on their business operations.

As the world faced a series of unexpected challenges—economic downturns, geopolitical tensions, and a global health crisis—the startup found itself navigating uncharted waters. The once-stable global marketplace became a volatile landscape, affecting supply chains, consumer behavior, and the overall stability of the e-commerce ecosystem.

Impact:

The consequences were immediate and far-reaching. The startup, unprepared for the magnitude of global events, faced disruptions in supply chains, logistics, and customer demand. The team struggled to adapt to the rapidly changing circumstances, and the once-thriving international platform faced a decline in user activity and revenue.

Elena, realizing the importance of resilience in the face of global uncertainties, attempted to pivot the startup's strategy. However, the lack of foresight had already impacted the startup's reputation and financial stability. The lesson learned was clear: global events can have a profound impact on business operations, and startups must incorporate resilience and contingency planning into their strategies to navigate the complexities of the global landscape.

The world is interconnected, and a startup's ability to thrive amidst global uncertainties requires a proactive approach to understanding and mitigating the potential risks associated with international business operations.

Neglecting the Well-Being of the Team

Chapter 20: The Burnout Epidemic

In the heart of Innovaria, a passionate team led by Daniel was on a mission to develop a revolutionary productivity tool. The startup culture thrived on ambition and dedication, with team members working long hours to meet ambitious deadlines. However, in the pursuit of success, Daniel inadvertently neglected the well-being of his team.

As the workload intensified and deadlines loomed, burnout became a prevalent issue within the startup. Team members, initially driven by passion, found themselves exhausted and demotivated. The consequences of neglecting their well-being were not just personal but had a ripple effect on the startup's productivity and creativity.

Impact:

The burnout epidemic led to a decline in overall team morale and a rise in employee turnover. The initial enthusiasm that fueled the startup's innovative spirit diminished, and the collaborative culture that once thrived turned into a breeding ground for stress and dissatisfaction.

Recognizing the toll on the team's well-being, Daniel attempted to implement wellness programs and flexible work arrangements. However, the initial oversight had already eroded trust and damaged the startup's reputation as a desirable workplace.

The lesson learned was profound: neglecting the well-being of the team is a costly mistake that can hinder a startup's ability to attract and retain top talent. Success isn't just about achieving milestones; it's about fostering a healthy and supportive work environment that allows individuals to thrive both personally and professionally.

Neglecting User Privacy in Data Handling

Chapter 21: The Trust Erosion

In the bustling tech hub of Innovaria, a team led by David set out to create a cutting-edge social media platform. Focused on delivering personalized user experiences, the startup collected vast amounts of user data without giving due consideration to privacy safeguards.

As the platform gained popularity, concerns about user privacy began to surface. The lack of transparent data-handling practices eroded trust among users. The once-loyal user base, now skeptical of the startup's commitment to privacy, started seeking alternative platforms that prioritized the protection of personal information.

Impact:

The consequences were swift and severe. Regulatory authorities took notice, and investigations into privacy violations ensued. Fines and legal battles drained the startup's resources. The tarnished reputation became a significant hurdle, making it difficult to attract new users and investors.

Realizing the gravity of the situation, David and his team implemented stringent privacy measures and communicated transparently with users. However, the damage had been done, and the startup faced an uphill battle to rebuild trust in an industry where privacy concerns loomed large.

The lesson learned was clear: neglecting user privacy can lead to a trust deficit that is challenging to overcome. In the age of data-driven technologies, startups must prioritize transparent data-handling practices to safeguard not only user information but also the long-term viability of their ventures.

Misjudging the Competitive Landscape

Chapter 22: The Blind Sprint

In the competitive arena of Innovaria, a team led by Sarah embarked on a mission to create a unique e-commerce platform catering to niche markets. Fueled by their vision, they focused intensely on developing distinctive features without thoroughly assessing the broader competitive landscape.

As the platform launched, Sarah realized they had misjudged the intensity of competition. Established players and agile startups had already captured the attention of the target audience, offering similar or even superior features. The blind sprint to launch had left Sarah's startup struggling to carve out a space in a crowded market.

IMPACT:

The consequences were evident as user acquisition lagged behind projections. Marketing efforts struggled to break through the noise, and the initial excitement waned. The misjudgment of the competitive landscape not only hindered user growth but also made it challenging to secure partnerships and investments.

Recognizing the oversight, Sarah and her team pivoted to differentiate the platform further and intensify marketing efforts. However, the initial miscalculation had set the startup on a more challenging path, navigating a fiercely competitive landscape that demanded not just innovation but strategic positioning.

The lesson learned was profound: success in the competitive landscape requires not just a great product but a comprehensive understanding of the market dynamics and competitors. Thorough market research and a strategic approach to differentiation are vital for startups aiming to thrive in crowded industries.

Underestimating the Importance of Customer Retention

Chapter 23: The Leaky Bucket Syndrome

In the heart of Innovaria, a team led by Olivia set out to disrupt the subscription box industry with a curated experience for enthusiasts. The startup focused intensely on acquiring new customers, offering enticing promotions and discounts. However, in the pursuit of expansion, they inadvertently neglected the crucial aspect of customer retention.

As the startup celebrated the influx of new subscribers, Olivia failed to notice the gradual leakage of existing customers. The initial excitement waned, and subscribers, without a compelling reason to stay, started churning. The leaky bucket syndrome had set in, and the startup faced a dual challenge of acquiring new customers and stemming the outflow of existing ones.

Impact:

The consequences were felt in the declining subscription renewals and recurring revenue. Olivia realized that the cost of acquiring new customers far exceeded the value gained from retaining existing ones. The oversight in customer retention not only impacted the startup's revenue stream but also tarnished its reputation as subscribers voiced their dissatisfaction.

Recognizing the importance of customer retention, Olivia implemented loyalty programs and personalized experiences to re-engage existing subscribers. However, the initial oversight had already impacted the startup's growth trajectory, highlighting the need for a balanced focus on both acquisition and retention from the outset.

The lesson learned was clear: while acquiring new customers is essential, underestimating the importance of customer retention can lead to a leaky bucket scenario that hinders a startup's sustainable growth. Success in subscription-based models requires a strategic and ongoing effort to keep existing customers satisfied and committed to the brand.

Overlooking the Impact of Cultural Sensitivity in Marketing

Chapter 24: The Tone-Deaf Campaign

In the diverse landscape of Innovaria, a team led by Miguel aimed to introduce a new lifestyle app designed for global users. Excitement filled the air as they rolled out a marketing campaign intended to resonate with a broad audience. However, in their enthusiasm, the team overlooked the critical element of cultural sensitivity.

As the campaign unfolded, Miguel received feedback that certain elements were perceived as culturally insensitive or even offensive by some segments of the target audience. The oversight in cultural sensitivity not only led to a backlash on social media but also jeopardized the startup's reputation and user trust.

Impact:

The consequences were swift and widespread. The startup faced public scrutiny, and potential users, put off by the insensitive campaign, turned to competitors with more culturally aware marketing strategies. Miguel and his team found themselves in damage control, issuing apologies and attempting to salvage the brand's image.

Realizing the importance of cultural sensitivity, Miguel reevaluated the marketing strategy, incorporating diverse perspectives and seeking input from cultural experts. However, the initial misstep had already left a lasting impact, emphasizing the need for startups to approach marketing with a keen awareness of cultural nuances.

The lesson learned was profound: the global marketplace requires more than a one-size-fits-all approach. Cultural sensitivity is not just a social responsibility but a strategic necessity. Overlooking it can lead to significant setbacks, highlighting the importance of considering diverse perspectives in all aspects of a startup's operations.

Failing to Establish a Clear Brand Identity

Chapter 25: The Identity Crisis

In a vibrant corner of Innovaria, a team led by Sophia set out to revolutionize the fashion industry with a unique e-commerce platform. Excitement surrounded the launch, and the team worked diligently to bring their vision to life. However, in their eagerness to appeal to a broad audience, they neglected to establish a clear and distinctive brand identity.

As the platform entered the market, users were met with a brand that seemed to lack a defined personality. The messaging was inconsistent, and the visual elements failed to convey a cohesive identity. The startup found itself grappling with an identity crisis that made it challenging to stand out in a crowded market.

Impact:

The consequences were evident in the struggle to build brand recognition and loyalty. Users, faced with a myriad of choices, found it difficult to connect with the brand on a deeper level. The absence of a clear brand identity not only hindered customer acquisition but also made it challenging to communicate the startup's values and unique selling propositions.

Recognizing the importance of a strong brand identity, Sophia and her team revisited their branding strategy. They worked on defining the brand's personality, streamlining visual elements, and ensuring consistency across all touchpoints. However, the initial lack of a clear identity had already delayed the establishment of a strong brand presence.

The lesson learned was clear: in a competitive market, a clear and consistent brand identity is a powerful tool for attracting and retaining customers. Failing to define it from the outset can lead to an uphill battle for brand recognition and differentiation.

Ignoring the Impact of Social Responsibility on Brand Perception

Chapter 26: The Blind Eye to Social Impact

In the socially conscious landscape of Innovaria, a team led by Alex set out to launch a sustainable lifestyle brand. Driven by a commitment to environmental responsibility, they created products with eco-friendly materials and ethical sourcing. However, in their focus on sustainability, they inadvertently overlooked the broader concept of social responsibility.

As the brand gained visibility, users began to scrutinize not only the environmental impact but also the brand's stance on social issues. The lack of a clear commitment to social responsibility left the startup vulnerable to criticism and raised questions about the authenticity of its values.

Impact:

The consequences were felt in the erosion of brand trust and the loss of potential customers who sought brands aligned with their social values. The startup faced negative publicity and found itself in a position where competitors with robust social responsibility initiatives overshadowed its presence.

Realizing the oversight, Alex and the team began to actively engage in social responsibility initiatives, from supporting local communities to advocating for social causes. However, the initial neglect had already impacted the brand's perception, emphasizing the importance of integrating social responsibility into a startup's core values from the start.

The lesson learned was clear: consumers increasingly value brands that not only prioritize environmental sustainability but also demonstrate a commitment to social responsibility. Ignoring this aspect can lead to a disconnect with socially conscious consumers and hinder the long-term success of a startup in a socially aware market.

Underestimating the Impact of Online Reviews on Reputation

Chapter 27: The Review Ripple Effect

In the digital marketplace of Innovaria, a team led by Jessica launched a platform connecting local service providers with customers. Excitement surrounded the platform's debut, but in their eagerness to gain users, they underestimated the impact of online reviews on the startup's reputation.

As the platform gained traction, user reviews began to shape its image. The team soon realized that negative reviews, even if few in number, had a disproportionate impact on the startup's reputation. The underestimation of the influence of online reviews led to a ripple effect that affected user trust and acquisition.

IMPACT:

The consequences were evident in the struggle to attract new service providers and users. The negative reviews, amplified by the interconnected nature of the online community, became a significant obstacle. Prospective users, influenced by the negative feedback, hesitated to engage with the platform, leading to a decline in overall user activity.

Recognizing the importance of managing online reviews, Jessica and her team implemented strategies to encourage positive feedback and address concerns promptly. However, the initial underestimation had already left a lasting impact on the startup's reputation, emphasizing the critical role that online reviews play in shaping public perception.

The lesson learned was clear: online reviews are a powerful force that can significantly impact a startup's reputation. Ignoring their influence or underestimating their importance can have far-reaching consequences on user trust and the overall success of the platform.

Overlooking the Impact of Employee Satisfaction on Productivity

Chapter 28: The Disengagement Dilemma

In a bustling workspace within Innovaria, a team led by Chris aimed to develop innovative educational technology. Focused on meeting ambitious milestones, Chris inadvertently overlooked the critical factor of employee satisfaction.

As the workload intensified, team members began to experience burnout and dissatisfaction. The lack of attention to their well-being led to disengagement, affecting the overall productivity and creativity within the startup. The disengagement dilemma became a significant hurdle in achieving the startup's goals.

Impact:

The consequences were profound. High levels of disengagement resulted in a decline in productivity, missed deadlines, and a strained team dynamic. The once-thriving startup culture eroded, leading to increased turnover and difficulty attracting top talent.

Realizing the impact of employee satisfaction on productivity, Chris implemented measures to improve the work environment, foster team collaboration, and address individual concerns. However, the initial oversight had already left scars on the startup's efficiency and culture.

The lesson learned was clear: the success of a startup is intricately tied to the satisfaction and engagement of its team members. Ignoring their well-being can lead to a disengagement dilemma that affects not only productivity but also the overall health of the startup's work culture.

Underestimating the Importance of Financial Literacy in Decision-Making

Chapter 29: The Fiscal Blind Spot

In the financial landscape of Innovaria, a team led by Ryan embarked on a mission to develop a financial planning app. While the startup was focused on helping users make informed financial decisions, the team inadvertently overlooked the critical aspect of financial literacy within their own ranks.

As the startup secured funding and navigated the complexities of budgeting, the lack of financial literacy among team members became evident. Decision-making processes were hampered, and financial mismanagement became a significant challenge. The fiscal blind spot had a cascading effect on the startup's stability and growth.

Impact:

The consequences were felt in budget overruns, inefficient resource allocation, and a lack of financial foresight. The startup struggled to weather financial challenges and attract further investment, as stakeholders questioned the team's ability to manage resources effectively.

Realizing the importance of financial literacy, Ryan and his team implemented training programs and sought external financial expertise. However, the initial oversight had already impacted the startup's financial health, emphasizing the critical role of financial literacy in making informed and sustainable business decisions.

The lesson learned was clear: financial literacy is not just a necessity for users of a financial planning app; it's an essential skill for the internal decision-makers within a startup. Ignoring this aspect can lead to a fiscal blind spot that hinders a startup's ability to navigate the intricate financial landscape.

Neglecting the Power of Storytelling in Marketing

Chapter 30: The Silent Narrative

In the storytelling realm of Innovaria, a team led by Emma set out to launch an innovative health and wellness app. Focused on the features and functionalities, the team inadvertently neglected the critical element of storytelling in their marketing strategy.

As the app entered the market, users were presented with a silent narrative. The startup failed to convey the compelling stories behind the development, the journey of the team, and the real-world impact of the app. The absence of a captivating narrative left the startup struggling to connect with its audience on an emotional level.

Impact:

The consequences were evident in the lack of user engagement and the struggle to differentiate the app from competitors. The silent narrative failed to create a memorable brand identity, and users were left with a functional but forgettable experience. The startup faced challenges in building brand loyalty and attracting a dedicated user base.

Realizing the oversight, Emma and her team revamped their marketing strategy to incorporate storytelling. They shared the inspiring stories behind the app's development, the challenges overcome by the team, and the positive impact on users' lives. However, the initial neglect had already created a gap in the startup's brand perception.

The lesson learned was clear: in the crowded marketplace, neglecting the power of storytelling can diminish a startup's ability to connect with users on a deeper level. Crafting and sharing compelling narratives can transform a product into a meaningful experience, fostering brand loyalty and emotional connections.

Overlooking the Importance of Accessibility in Product Design

Chapter 31: The Inclusive Oversight

In the design-centric hub of Innovaria, a team led by Jordan aimed to create a revolutionary communication app. Focused on cutting-edge features, the team inadvertently overlooked the crucial aspect of accessibility in their product design.

As the app gained popularity, feedback from users with diverse abilities pointed to accessibility challenges. The oversight in considering the needs of all users led to a portion of the audience facing difficulties in navigating and utilizing the app effectively. The inclusive oversight became a stumbling block for the startup's mission to revolutionize communication for everyone.

Impact:

The consequences were felt in user dissatisfaction, negative reviews, and a tarnished reputation. The startup faced criticism for its failure to provide an inclusive user experience, and potential users with accessibility needs turned to competitors offering more accessible solutions. The oversight became a barrier to the startup's goal of creating a widely embraced communication platform.

Recognizing the importance of accessibility, Jordan and the team worked to redesign the app with inclusivity in mind. They sought input from users with diverse abilities and collaborated with accessibility experts. However, the initial oversight had already impacted the startup's standing in the market.

The lesson learned was clear: accessibility is not just a checkbox in product design; it's a fundamental aspect that ensures the inclusivity of the user experience. Overlooking this critical element can lead to exclusion, limiting a startup's reach and potential impact.

Underestimating the Impact of Regulatory Compliance on Business Operations

Chapter 32: The Regulatory Quagmire

In the regulatory landscape of Innovaria, a team led by Taylor ventured into the realm of financial technology with an innovative payment platform. Focused on technological advancements, the team inadvertently underestimated the impact of regulatory compliance on their business operations.

As the platform gained users, regulatory authorities took notice of potential compliance gaps. The oversight in thoroughly understanding and adhering to regulations led to legal challenges, fines, and disruptions in business operations. The regulatory quagmire became a significant obstacle for the startup's growth.

Impact:

The consequences were severe, with legal battles draining the startup's resources and causing reputational damage. Users, concerned about the security and legality of the platform, started to lose trust. The startup found itself entangled in a regulatory web that not only hindered expansion but also jeopardized its very existence.

Recognizing the importance of regulatory compliance, Taylor and the team engaged legal experts, revised their operations to meet regulatory standards, and implemented robust compliance measures. However, the initial underestimation had already left a lasting impact on the startup's financial health and standing in the market.

The lesson learned was clear: in industries governed by regulations, underestimating the impact of compliance can lead to legal challenges that pose a significant threat to a startup's survival. Proactive efforts to understand, anticipate, and comply with regulations are essential for long-term sustainability.

Overlooking the Significance of Network Building in Entrepreneurship

Chapter 33: The Isolated Endeavor

In the entrepreneurial landscape of Innovaria, a team led by Morgan embarked on a mission to develop a groundbreaking artificial intelligence platform. Focused on technical innovation, they inadvertently overlooked the significance of network building and relationship building within the industry.

As the startup progressed, Morgan realized the isolation had consequences beyond the technical realm. The lack of a robust professional network meant missed opportunities for partnerships, mentorship, and valuable insights. The isolated endeavor hindered the startup's growth potential and access to critical resources.

Impact:

The consequences were evident in the challenges faced in securing partnerships, attracting top talent, and staying informed about industry trends. The startup struggled to navigate the complex entrepreneurial landscape, and competitors with stronger networks gained a competitive edge.

Recognizing the oversight, Morgan and the team actively engaged in networking events, industry conferences, and mentorship programs. However, the initial isolation had already delayed the startup's progress and hindered its ability to capitalize on strategic opportunities.

The lesson learned was clear: entrepreneurship is not just a technical endeavor; it's a collaborative and interconnected journey. Overlooking the significance of network building can limit a startup's access to valuable resources, insights, and partnerships that are crucial for sustained success.

Neglecting the Importance of Agile and Adaptive Leadership

Chapter 34: The Rigidity Trap

In the dynamic ecosystem of Innovaria, a team led by Casey set out to create a versatile project management tool. Focused on developing robust features, Casey inadvertently neglected the importance of agile and adaptive leadership in steering the startup through evolving challenges.

As the market shifted and user needs evolved, the rigid leadership approach became a hindrance. The startup struggled to pivot in response to changing dynamics, and decision-making processes became slow and inflexible. The rigidity trap impeded the startup's ability to navigate the ever-changing landscape.

Impact:

The consequences were evident in missed opportunities, delayed responses to market trends, and a decline in user engagement. Competitors with agile leadership seized emerging opportunities, leaving Casey's startup grappling with the consequences of a leadership style that failed to adapt to the fast-paced nature of the industry.

Recognizing the importance of agile and adaptive leadership, Casey and the team implemented strategies to foster a more flexible decision-making process. However, the initial rigidity had already created challenges in maintaining a competitive edge and responding effectively to market shifts.

The lesson learned was clear: leadership in the startup world requires not only technical expertise but also agility and adaptability. Neglecting this aspect can lead to a rigidity trap that hampers a startup's ability to innovate, pivot, and thrive in a dynamic environment.

Underestimating the Impact of Diversity and Inclusion on Innovation

Chapter 35: The Innovation Blind Spot

In the diverse and inclusive environment of Innovaria, a team led by Jordan aimed to create cutting-edge artificial intelligence solutions. While the startup acknowledged the importance of innovation, they inadvertently underestimated the impact of diversity and inclusion on the creative process.

As the team worked on ground breaking projects, Jordan noticed a lack of diverse perspectives in decision-making. The innovation blind spot became evident when the solutions developed failed to resonate with a broader audience. The oversight in fostering diversity and inclusion hindered the startup's ability to tap into a wealth of varied experiences and insights.

Impact:

The consequences were felt in the limited scope of innovation, missed market opportunities, and a lack of resonance with diverse user groups. Competitors with more inclusive teams showcased a broader range of perspectives in their products, leaving Jordan's startup at a disadvantage in the rapidly evolving landscape.

Recognizing the importance of diversity and inclusion, Jordan and the team implemented strategies to foster a more inclusive workplace, actively seeking diverse talent and encouraging a culture that values varied perspectives. However, the initial oversight had already created challenges in achieving innovation that resonated with a diverse user base.

The lesson learned was clear: diversity and inclusion are not just moral imperatives; they are essential catalysts for innovation. Neglecting this impact can lead to an innovation blind spot that hampers a startup's ability to create solutions that resonate with the diverse needs of a global audience.

Overlooking the Role of Emotional Intelligence in Leadership

Chapter 36: The Emotional Void

In the leadership domain of Innovaria, a team led by Taylor ventured into the development of advanced cybersecurity solutions. Focused on technical prowess, Taylor inadvertently overlooked the critical role of emotional intelligence in effective leadership.

As the startup faced challenges and uncertainties, the absence of emotional intelligence in leadership became apparent. Team members struggled with motivation, communication breakdowns increased, and the overall work environment became tense. The emotional void hindered the team's ability to navigate the complex landscape of cybersecurity innovation.

Impact:

The consequences were evident in decreased team morale, increased turnover, and challenges in fostering a collaborative culture. The startup faced difficulties in retaining top talent and attracting new team members who sought a supportive and emotionally intelligent work environment.

Recognizing the importance of emotional intelligence, Taylor and the leadership team underwent training to develop their emotional intelligence skills. Strategies were implemented to foster a more supportive and empathetic workplace. However, the initial oversight had already left an impact on the startup's team dynamics and overall effectiveness.

The lesson learned was clear: leadership is not just about technical proficiency; it's also about understanding and navigating the emotional landscape of a team. Overlooking the role of emotional intelligence can create an emotional void that hampers a startup's ability to build a resilient, motivated, and high-performing team.

Neglecting the Impact of Cybersecurity on Customer Trust

Chapter 37: The Trust Breach

In the technologically advanced arena of Innovaria, a team led by Alex set out to develop a state-of-the-art cloud storage platform. Focused on functionality and convenience, the team inadvertently neglected to prioritize the robustness of their cybersecurity measures.

As the platform gained users, cybersecurity concerns emerged. Instances of data breaches and unauthorized access eroded customer trust. The neglect of cybersecurity not only compromised user data but also tarnished the startup's reputation as a secure and reliable storage solution.

Impact:

The consequences were severe, with a decline in user trust and an exodus of customers to more secure alternatives. The startup faced legal challenges, reputational damage, and the costly process of rebuilding its cybersecurity infrastructure. The trust breach became a significant obstacle to the startup's mission of providing a secure cloud storage solution.

Realizing the impact, Alex and the team invested in enhancing cybersecurity measures, conducting thorough audits, and implementing encryption protocols. However, the initial neglect had already led to a loss of customer trust and a challenging path to rebuilding the startup's credibility.

The lesson learned was clear: in the digital age, neglecting the impact of cybersecurity on customer trust can have far-reaching consequences. Prioritizing robust security measures is not only a technical necessity but a fundamental element in building and maintaining the trust of users in a technology-driven product or service.

Underestimating the Power of Continuous Learning in Innovation

Chapter 38: The Knowledge Stagnation

In the ever-evolving landscape of Innovaria, a team led by Morgan embarked on a mission to develop cutting-edge artificial intelligence applications. Focused on initial success, the team inadvertently underestimated the importance of continuous learning in fostering innovation.

As the industry progressed and new technologies emerged, the startup found itself falling behind. The lack of a culture of continuous learning hindered the team's ability to adapt to the latest trends, incorporate new methodologies, and stay at the forefront of innovation. The knowledge stagnation became a significant barrier to the startup's competitiveness.

Impact:

The consequences were evident in outdated technologies, reduced competitiveness, and challenges in attracting top talent. Competitors with a commitment to continuous learning showcased a dynamic and innovative approach, leaving Morgan's startup struggling to keep up with the pace of industry advancements.

Recognizing the importance of continuous learning, Morgan implemented training programs, encouraged professional development, and fostered a culture of curiosity and exploration within the team. However, the initial underestimation had already led to a knowledge gap that required dedicated efforts to bridge.

The lesson learned was clear: innovation is not a one-time achievement but an ongoing process that requires a commitment to continuous learning. Underestimating the power of staying abreast of industry developments can lead to knowledge stagnation, hindering a startup's ability to remain innovative and competitive.

Ignoring the Impact of Company Culture on Employee Engagement

Chapter 39: The Cultural Disconnect

In the vibrant work environment of Innovaria, a team led by Taylor set out to develop groundbreaking augmented reality applications. Focused on technical achievements, the team inadvertently ignored the impact of company culture on employee engagement.

As the workload increased, team members felt a growing disconnect with the company culture. The lack of a supportive and inclusive atmosphere led to decreased morale, lower levels of commitment, and challenges in retaining top talent. The cultural disconnect became a significant hurdle in fostering a collaborative and innovative work environment.

Impact:

The consequences were evident in increased turnover, difficulties in attracting new talent, and a decline in overall productivity. Competitors with a strong and positive company culture showcased higher levels of employee engagement and creativity, leaving Taylor's startup at a disadvantage in the talent market.

Recognizing the importance of company culture, Taylor and the leadership team worked to redefine and strengthen the cultural pillars of the startup. Initiatives were implemented to foster inclusivity, communication, and a sense of belonging. However, the initial cultural disconnect had already left its mark on the startup's team dynamics and effectiveness.

The lesson learned was clear: company culture is a powerful force that influences employee engagement, innovation, and overall success. Ignoring its impact can lead to a cultural disconnect that hampers a startup's ability to attract, retain, and inspire a high-performing team.

Underestimating the Role of Marketing in Educating Customers

Chapter 40: The Information Void

In the competitive marketplace of Innovaria, a team led by Alex aimed to launch a revolutionary health and fitness app. Focused on the app's features and functionalities, the team inadvertently underestimated the crucial role of marketing in educating customers about the app's value proposition.

As the app hit the market, potential users faced an information void. The startup assumed that the innovative features would speak for themselves, neglecting the need to proactively educate customers on how to maximize the app's benefits. The result was confusion, underutilization of features, and a lack of understanding about the app's unique offerings.

Impact:

The consequences were evident in low user engagement, negative reviews due to misunderstanding, and challenges in building a dedicated user base. Competitors with robust marketing strategies effectively communicated their value propositions, leaving Alex's startup struggling to convey the full potential of their innovative app.

Realizing the oversight, Alex and the marketing team implemented targeted campaigns to educate users about the app's features, benefits, and unique selling points. However, the initial underestimation had already led to missed opportunities and a slower adoption rate.

The lesson learned was clear: innovation alone is not enough; effective marketing is essential to educate customers about the value a product or service brings. Underestimating the role of marketing in customer education can result in an information void that hinders a startup's ability to showcase its unique offerings.

Overlooking the Importance of Mental Health and Well-being in the Workplace

Chapter 41: The Well-being Blind Spot

In the bustling workspace of Innovaria, a team led by Morgan aimed to develop groundbreaking applications for remote collaboration. Focused on productivity and innovation, the team inadvertently overlooked the critical importance of mental health and well-being in the workplace.

As the demands of the startup environment intensified, team members began to experience burnout, stress, and a decline in mental well-being. The well-being blind spot became evident as productivity waned, and the overall work atmosphere became strained. The neglect of mental health had a significant impact on the team's overall performance.

IMPACT:

The consequences were felt in increased absenteeism, decreased team morale, and challenges in retaining talent. The startup struggled to maintain a positive and collaborative work environment, leading to difficulties in attracting new team members who sought a workplace that prioritized mental health.

Recognizing the importance of mental health, Morgan and the leadership team implemented well-being programs, offered mental health resources, and fostered an open culture around mental health discussions. However, the initial oversight had already impacted the startup's team dynamics and hindered its ability to create a thriving and sustainable workplace.

The lesson learned was clear: a focus on productivity and innovation should not come at the expense of employee well-being. Overlooking the importance of mental health can lead to a well-being blind spot that affects team performance, retention, and the overall health of the workplace.

Neglecting the Impact of Sustainability Practices on Brand Image

Chapter 42: The Green Oversight

In the environmentally conscious landscape of Innovaria, a team led by Taylor set out to develop a series of innovative smart devices. Focused on technological advancements, the team inadvertently neglected to prioritize sustainability practices in their product development and business operations.

As the startup gained visibility, environmentally conscious consumers scrutinized the lack of sustainable practices. The green oversight became evident as the startup faced criticism for contributing to environmental issues rather than alleviating them. The neglect of sustainability had a detrimental impact on the startup's brand image

Impact:

The consequences were severe, with a decline in customer trust, negative publicity, and challenges in attracting a growing segment of eco-conscious consumers. Competitors with robust sustainability practices showcased a commitment to environmental responsibility, leaving Taylor's startup struggling to repair its damaged brand image.

Realizing the oversight, Taylor and the team implemented sustainable practices in product design, sourcing, and operations. However, the initial neglect had already led to reputational damage and a loss of credibility in the eyes of environmentally conscious consumers.

The lesson learned was clear: in an era where sustainability is a key consideration for consumers, neglecting the impact of sustainability practices on brand image can have far-reaching consequences. Prioritizing sustainable and eco-friendly initiatives is not just an ethical choice; it's a strategic necessity for building and maintaining a positive brand image.

Underestimating the Importance of Crisis Preparedness in Business Operations

Chapter 43: The Crisis Unready

In the dynamic landscape of Innovaria, a team led by Alex set out to disrupt the market with a cutting-edge e-commerce platform. Focused on rapid growth, the team inadvertently underestimated the importance of crisis preparedness in their business operations.

As the startup gained momentum, unforeseen challenges emerged. The absence of a comprehensive crisis preparedness plan left the team scrambling to address issues such as cybersecurity threats, supply chain disruptions, and unexpected market downturns. The crisis unready approach hindered the startup's ability to navigate turbulent times effectively.

Impact:

The consequences were severe, with disruptions in business continuity, financial losses, and reputational damage. Competitors with robust crisis preparedness plans showcased resilience in the face of challenges, leaving Alex's startup at a disadvantage in the market.

Recognizing the importance of crisis preparedness, Alex and the leadership team implemented a comprehensive plan, covering various potential scenarios. However, the initial underestimation had already led to setbacks, emphasizing the critical role of being proactive and prepared for crises in the unpredictable business landscape.

The lesson learned was clear: unforeseen challenges are an inevitable part of business, and underestimating the importance of crisis preparedness can have lasting impacts. Prioritizing a well-defined and agile crisis response strategy is essential for a startup's ability to weather uncertainties and emerge stronger.

Overlooking the Role of Emotional Resilience in Leadership

Chapter 44: The Resilience Gap

In the challenging entrepreneurial landscape of Innovaria, a team led by Taylor set out to develop innovative solutions in artificial intelligence. Focused on technical expertise, the team inadvertently overlooked the crucial role of emotional resilience in leadership.

As the startup faced setbacks and unexpected challenges, the absence of emotional resilience became apparent. Team members struggled to cope with stress, and the overall team morale suffered. The resilience gap hindered the leadership's ability to inspire and guide the team through turbulent times.

Impact:

The consequences were evident in increased turnover, decreased productivity, and challenges in maintaining a positive work environment. Competitors with emotionally resilient leadership showcased the ability to navigate challenges effectively, leaving Taylor's startup grappling with the effects of a leadership resilience gap.

Recognizing the importance of emotional resilience, Taylor and the leadership team underwent training to develop their emotional intelligence and resilience skills. Strategies were implemented to foster a supportive and resilient work culture. However, the initial oversight had already left an impact on the startup's team dynamics.

The lesson learned was clear: leadership in the entrepreneurial journey requires not only technical acumen but also emotional resilience. Overlooking the role of emotional resilience can create a resilience gap that hampers a startup's ability to navigate challenges and maintain a motivated and engaged team.

Underestimating the Importance of Customer Feedback in Product Development

Chapter 45: The Feedback Void

In the customer-centric realm of Innovaria, a team led by Morgan set out to develop a groundbreaking mobile application for social networking. Focused on technical innovation, the team inadvertently underestimated the importance of actively seeking and incorporating customer feedback in their product development process.

As the app launched, the team assumed that its innovative features would automatically resonate with users. The feedback void became evident when users faced challenges and the app failed to meet their evolving needs. The neglect of customer feedback hindered the startup's ability to create a product aligned with user expectations.

IMPACT:

The consequences were evident in low user retention, negative reviews, and challenges in attracting new users. Competitors that actively sought and incorporated customer feedback showcased a more user-centric approach, leaving Morgan's startup struggling to bridge the gap between their vision and user expectations.

Realizing the importance of customer feedback, Morgan and the team implemented robust feedback mechanisms, conducted user surveys, and actively engaged with the user community. However, the initial neglect had already led to missed opportunities and a slower adoption rate.

The lesson learned was clear: innovation should be a collaborative effort with customers, and underestimating the importance of customer feedback can result in a feedback void that hinders a startup's ability to create a product that truly resonates with its target audience.

Neglecting the Impact of Employee Well-being on Organizational Success

Chapter 46: The Well-being Oversight

In the fast-paced organizational landscape of Innovaria, a team led by Alex ventured into the development of cutting-edge artificial intelligence solutions. Focused on achieving ambitious goals, the team inadvertently overlooked the impact of employee well-being on the overall success of the organization.

As the workload intensified, team members faced burnout, stress, and a decline in mental health. The well-being oversight became apparent as productivity waned, and the overall team morale suffered. Neglecting employee well-being hindered the startup's ability to maintain a positive and sustainable work environment.

Impact:

The consequences were evident in increased absenteeism, higher turnover rates, and challenges in attracting top talent. Competitors with a focus on employee well-being showcased a more resilient and motivated workforce, leaving Alex's startup at a disadvantage in the talent market.

Recognizing the importance of employee well-being, Alex and the leadership team implemented well-being programs, flexible work arrangements, and initiatives to support mental health. However, the initial oversight had already left an impact on the startup's organizational success and team dynamics.

The lesson learned was clear: organizational success is intricately linked to the well-being of its employees. Neglecting the impact of employee well-being can lead to a well-being oversight that hampers a startup's ability to attract, retain, and nurture a high-performing team.

Underestimating the Power of Networking in Business Growth

Chapter 47: The Networking Gap

In the interconnected business landscape of Innovaria, a team led by Taylor ventured into the development of innovative software solutions. Focused on technical excellence, the team inadvertently underestimated the power of networking in driving business growth.

As the startup aimed to expand its reach and partnerships, the absence of a robust networking strategy became evident. The networking gap hindered the team's ability to forge valuable connections, explore collaborative opportunities, and stay informed about industry trends. Neglecting networking efforts became a barrier to the startup's growth potential.

Impact:

The consequences were evident in missed partnership opportunities, difficulties in securing funding, and challenges in staying competitive. Competitors with a strong networking presence showcased a broader reach and a more informed approach to business strategies, leaving Taylor's startup at a disadvantage in the market.

Recognizing the importance of networking, Taylor and the team actively engaged in industry events, joined professional networks, and fostered relationships with key stakeholders. However, the initial underestimation had already led to missed opportunities and a slower pace of business growth.

The lesson learned was clear: in the business world, networking is not just a supplementary activity but a strategic imperative for growth. Underestimating the power of networking can result in a networking gap that hampers a startup's ability to capitalize on opportunities and navigate the complex dynamics of the industry.

Overlooking the Role of Innovation in Addressing Market Trends

Chapter 48: The Trend Blindness

In the ever-evolving market of Innovaria, a team led by Morgan sought to create groundbreaking solutions in augmented reality. Focused on current market demands, the team inadvertently overlooked the critical role of innovation in addressing emerging trends.

As market trends shifted, the startup found itself struggling to adapt. The trend blindness became evident as competitors introduced innovative features and products that resonated with the evolving needs of consumers. Neglecting the proactive pursuit of innovation hindered the startup's ability to stay ahead in a rapidly changing market.

Impact:

The consequences were evident in reduced market share, declining user interest, and challenges in maintaining a competitive edge. Competitors that actively embraced innovation showcased a more responsive approach to market trends, leaving Morgan's startup at a disadvantage in the fast-paced industry.

Recognizing the importance of innovation, Morgan and the team implemented processes to stay informed about emerging trends, fostered a culture of creativity, and prioritized R&D efforts. However, the initial oversight had already led to missed opportunities and a diminished position in the market.

The lesson learned was clear: market trends are not static, and innovation is crucial for staying relevant. Overlooking the role of innovation in addressing market trends can result in trend blindness, hindering a startup's ability to meet evolving consumer expectations and maintain market leadership.

Underestimating the Importance of Cybersecurity in Protecting Intellectual Property

Chapter 49: The Security Gap

In the digitally-driven domain of Innovaria, a team led by Alex delved into creating cutting-edge artificial intelligence algorithms. Focused on technological advancements, the team inadvertently underestimated the critical importance of cybersecurity in safeguarding their intellectual property.

As the startup's algorithms gained attention, the security gap became evident. The lack of robust cybersecurity measures left the intellectual property vulnerable to theft and unauthorized access. Neglecting cybersecurity measures became a significant risk to the startup's proprietary technology.

Impact:

The consequences were severe, with instances of intellectual property theft, compromised algorithms, and challenges in maintaining a competitive advantage. Competitors with a strong focus on cybersecurity showcased a commitment to protecting their innovations, leaving Alex's startup grappling with the aftermath of security breaches.

Realizing the importance of cybersecurity, Alex and the team implemented encryption protocols, secure access controls, and regular security audits. However, the initial underestimation had already led to compromised intellectual property and reputational damage.

The lesson learned was clear: in a technology-driven landscape, underestimating the importance of cybersecurity can have far-reaching consequences on the protection of intellectual property. Prioritizing robust cybersecurity measures is not only a technical necessity but a strategic imperative for safeguarding proprietary innovations.

Neglecting the Role of Ethical Considerations in Technological Innovation

Chapter 50: The Ethical Void

In the ethically conscious landscape of Innovaria, a team led by Taylor endeavored to develop groundbreaking applications in biotechnology. Focused on technological advancements, the team inadvertently neglected the crucial role of ethical considerations in their innovation process.

As the startup's technologies reached the market, ethical concerns arose. The ethical void became evident when users questioned the potential societal impact, data privacy issues, and ethical implications of the biotechnological advancements. Neglecting ethical considerations became a significant challenge for the startup's reputation and user trust.

Impact:

The consequences were severe, with public scrutiny, legal challenges, and a tarnished brand image. Competitors that actively incorporated ethical considerations in their innovation process showcased a commitment to responsible technology, leaving Taylor's startup facing reputational damage and a loss of user trust.

Recognizing the importance of ethical considerations, Taylor and the team implemented ethical frameworks, engaged in transparent communication about the societal impact of their technologies, and sought external ethical assessments. However, the initial neglect had already led to reputational challenges and the need for extensive efforts to rebuild trust.

The lesson learned was clear: technological innovation must go hand in hand with ethical considerations. Neglecting the role of ethics in innovation can lead to an ethical void that jeopardizes a startup's reputation, user trust, and long-term success in the market.

Ignoring the Impact of Global Economic Trends on Business Strategy:

Chapter 51: The Economic Blind Spot

In the ever-changing global landscape of Innovaria, a team led by Morgan ventured into the development of advanced financial technology solutions. Focused on technical innovation, the team inadvertently ignored the potential impact of global economic trends on their business strategy.

As economic conditions shifted, the startup found itself vulnerable to unforeseen challenges. The economic blind spot became evident when the team struggled to adapt its business model to economic fluctuations, leading to financial instability and market uncertainties.

Impact:

The consequences were evident in revenue fluctuations, difficulties in securing funding, and challenges in maintaining a sustainable business model. Competitors with a keen awareness of global economic trends showcased a more adaptive approach, leaving Morgan's startup grappling with the effects of an economic blind spot.

Recognizing the importance of economic foresight, Morgan and the team implemented strategies to monitor and adapt to global economic trends actively. However, the initial oversight had already led to setbacks and a need for strategic realignment.

The lesson learned was clear: global economic trends can significantly impact business strategy, and ignoring this factor can result in an economic blind spot. Prioritizing economic awareness and adaptability is essential for a startup's resilience in a dynamic and interconnected business environment.

Underestimating the Importance of Data Privacy in User Trust

Chapter 52: The Privacy Gap

In the era of data-driven technology in Innovaria, a team led by Taylor set out to develop a cutting-edge artificial intelligence platform. Focused on technological advancements, the team inadvertently underestimated the critical importance of data privacy in building and maintaining user trust.

As the platform gained users, concerns about data privacy emerged. The privacy gap became evident when users questioned how their data was collected, stored, and utilized. Neglecting to prioritize robust data privacy measures not only exposed the startup to legal challenges but also eroded user trust.

Impact:

The consequences were severe, with a decline in user trust, legal repercussions, and challenges in attracting new users. Competitors with a strong focus on data privacy showcased a commitment to protecting user information, leaving Taylor's startup struggling to rebuild trust and implement comprehensive data privacy measures.

Realizing the importance of data privacy, Taylor and the team implemented encryption protocols, transparent privacy policies, and regular security audits. However, the initial underestimation had already led to reputational damage and the need for extensive efforts to regain user confidence.

The lesson learned was clear: in the digital age, underestimating the importance of data privacy can have significant consequences on user trust and the overall success of a technology-driven platform. Prioritizing robust data privacy measures is not only a legal requirement but a foundational element in building and maintaining a positive user relationship.

Neglecting the Significance of Employee Training in Cybersecurity

Chapter 53: The Knowledge Gap

In the technologically driven landscape of Innovaria, a team led by Alex delved into the development of innovative cybersecurity solutions. Focused on cutting-edge technologies, the team inadvertently neglected the significance of ongoing employee training in cybersecurity.

As the startup's operations expanded, the knowledge gap among employees became evident. The lack of comprehensive cybersecurity training left the team vulnerable to social engineering attacks, phishing attempts, and other cyber threats. Neglecting employee training in cybersecurity not only exposed the startup to potential breaches but also hindered the overall security posture.

Impact:

The consequences were severe, with instances of data breaches, compromised systems, and reputational damage. Competitors with robust employee training programs showcased a more resilient defense against cyber threats, leaving Alex's startup at a disadvantage in the cybersecurity landscape.

Recognizing the importance of employee training, Alex and the leadership team implemented regular cybersecurity awareness programs, simulated phishing exercises, and provided ongoing education on the latest cyber threats. However, the initial neglect had already led to security incidents that required extensive remediation efforts.

The lesson learned was clear: cybersecurity is a shared responsibility, and neglecting the significance of employee training creates a knowledge gap that exposes a startup to preventable security risks. Prioritizing ongoing education and awareness is essential for building a cybersecurity-aware culture within the organization.

Overlooking the Role of Environmental Sustainability in Corporate Responsibility

Chapter 54: The Sustainability Oversight

In the era of heightened environmental awareness in Innovaria, a team led by Morgan ventured into the development of innovative smart devices. Focused on technological advancements, the team inadvertently overlooked the critical role of environmental sustainability in corporate responsibility.

As the smart devices gained popularity, concerns about their environmental impact arose. The sustainability oversight became evident when stakeholders, including customers and investors, questioned the startup's commitment to eco-friendly practices. Neglecting environmental sustainability not only posed ethical challenges but also hindered the startup's corporate responsibility efforts.

Impact:

The consequences were evident in reputational damage, decreased customer trust, and challenges in securing investments. Competitors with a strong emphasis on environmental sustainability showcased a commitment to responsible business practices, leaving Morgan's startup facing scrutiny and the need to implement sustainable initiatives.

Realizing the importance of environmental responsibility, Morgan and the team implemented eco-friendly practices in product design, manufacturing, and packaging. However, the initial oversight had already led to reputational challenges and the need for the startup to actively communicate and demonstrate its commitment to environmental sustainability.

The lesson learned was clear: in a socially conscious business environment, overlooking the role of environmental sustainability in corporate responsibility can have significant consequences. Prioritizing eco-friendly practices is not just a moral obligation but a strategic imperative for building a positive brand image and maintaining stakeholder trust.

Underestimating the Impact of Social Media in Shaping Brand Perception

Chapter 55: The Social Media Blindness

In the interconnected world of Innovaria, a team led by Taylor set out to revolutionize the e-commerce sector. Focused on product development and customer experience, the team inadvertently underestimated the powerful impact of social media in shaping brand perception.

As the startup launched its e-commerce platform, discussions on social media platforms played a pivotal role in shaping public opinion. The social media blindness became evident when negative sentiments and customer grievances went unaddressed, leading to a tarnished brand image. Neglecting the influence of social media not only affected customer trust but also hindered the startup's ability to control its narrative.

Impact:

The consequences were severe, with a decline in customer loyalty, negative online reviews, and challenges in attracting new users. Competitors with a proactive social media strategy showcased a more engaged and responsive approach, leaving Taylor's startup struggling to mitigate the impact of the social media blindness.

Realizing the importance of social media, Taylor and the marketing team actively engaged with customers on various platforms, addressed concerns promptly, and leveraged social media as a tool for brand building. However, the initial underestimation had already led to reputational damage that required dedicated efforts to repair.

The lesson learned was clear: social media is a powerful force that can shape brand perception, and underestimating its impact constitutes a social media blindness that can have lasting consequences. Actively managing and leveraging social media is essential for startups to build a positive brand image and maintain a strong online presence.

Neglecting the Importance of Agility in Business Operations

Chapter 56: The Rigidity Trap

In the dynamic business landscape of Innovaria, a team led by Alex aimed to establish a groundbreaking e-commerce platform. Focused on initial success and structured processes, the team inadvertently neglected the importance of agility in their business operations.

As market demands evolved, the rigidity trap became evident. The startup found it challenging to adapt quickly to changing customer preferences, emerging technologies, and unforeseen challenges. Neglecting agility in business operations not only hindered the startup's responsiveness but also limited its ability to stay competitive.

Impact:

The consequences were evident in missed opportunities, slow response to market changes, and difficulties in meeting customer expectations. Competitors with agile business operations showcased a more adaptive approach, leaving Alex's startup at a disadvantage in the fast-paced e-commerce sector.

Recognizing the importance of agility, Alex and the leadership team implemented flexible processes, embraced a culture of continuous improvement, and fostered an environment that encouraged innovation and adaptability. However, the initial neglect had already led to setbacks that required strategic realignment.

The lesson learned was clear: in a rapidly changing business environment, neglecting the importance of agility can result in a rigidity trap that limits a startup's ability to navigate uncertainties and capitalize on emerging opportunities. Prioritizing agility in business operations is essential for maintaining a competitive edge and ensuring long-term success.

Underestimating the Role of Diversity in Driving Innovation

Chapter 57: The Diversity Gap

In the innovative ecosystem of Innovaria, a team led by Morgan set out to develop cutting-edge solutions in artificial intelligence. Focused on technical prowess, the team inadvertently underestimated the crucial role of diversity in driving innovation.

As the startup faced complex challenges, the diversity gap became evident. A lack of diverse perspectives and experiences hindered the team's ability to generate creative solutions, resulting in a narrower range of ideas and approaches. Neglecting diversity not only limited innovation but also created challenges in attracting top talent from diverse backgrounds.

IMPACT:

The consequences were evident in a lack of creative solutions, difficulties in problem-solving, and challenges in fostering an inclusive work culture. Competitors with diverse teams showcased a more robust innovation pipeline, leaving Morgan's startup at a disadvantage in the rapidly evolving field of artificial intelligence.

Recognizing the importance of diversity, Morgan and the leadership team implemented initiatives to foster a diverse and inclusive workplace, actively sought talent from various backgrounds, and promoted a culture of collaboration. However, the initial neglect had already led to missed opportunities and a less dynamic approach to innovation.

The lesson learned was clear: diversity is a driving force behind innovation, and underestimating its role creates a diversity gap that hampers a startup's ability to excel in a rapidly changing landscape. Prioritizing diversity and inclusion is not just a moral imperative but a strategic necessity for fostering innovation and staying competitive.

Neglecting the Importance of Customer Retention in Growth Strategies

Chapter 58: The Retention Oversight

In the competitive market of Innovaria, a team led by Taylor aimed to establish a revolutionary subscription-based service. Focused on acquiring new customers, the team inadvertently neglected the crucial importance of customer retention in their growth strategies.

As the startup celebrated initial successes in customer acquisition, the retention oversight became evident. The emphasis on acquiring new customers overshadowed efforts to retain existing ones, leading to a high churn rate. Neglecting customer retention not only resulted in lost revenue but also made it challenging to build a loyal customer base.

Impact:

The consequences were evident in declining revenue, increased customer acquisition costs, and challenges in maintaining a sustainable business model. Competitors with a focus on customer retention showcased a more stable growth trajectory, leaving Taylor's startup struggling to bridge the gap and retain a loyal customer base.

Recognizing the importance of customer retention, Taylor and the team implemented loyalty programs, personalized customer experiences, and strategies to address customer feedback. However, the initial oversight had already led to financial setbacks and the need for a comprehensive customer retention strategy.

The lesson learned was clear: customer retention is as vital as customer acquisition in sustaining business growth, and neglecting its importance creates a retention oversight that can impede a startup's long-term success. Prioritizing customer satisfaction and retention strategies is essential for building a resilient and profitable business.

Underestimating the Impact of Corporate Culture on Employee Productivity

Chapter 59: The Culture Gap

In the collaborative workspace of Innovaria, a team led by Alex embarked on creating a dynamic fintech platform. Focused on technical excellence, the team inadvertently underestimated the profound impact of corporate culture on employee productivity.

As the startup grew, the culture gap became evident. The lack of a cohesive and positive corporate culture led to challenges in team collaboration, communication breakdowns, and a decline in employee morale. Neglecting the impact of corporate culture not only affected the work environment but also hindered overall employee productivity.

Impact:

The consequences were evident in increased turnover rates, difficulties in attracting top talent, and challenges in maintaining a motivated workforce. Competitors with a strong and positive corporate culture showcased higher employee satisfaction and productivity, leaving Alex's startup at a disadvantage in the talent market.

Recognizing the importance of corporate culture, Alex and the leadership team implemented initiatives to foster a positive work environment, encourage open communication, and align values across the organization. However, the initial underestimation had already led to cultural challenges that required dedicated efforts to reshape.

The lesson learned was clear: corporate culture plays a significant role in employee productivity and overall organizational success. Underestimating its impact creates a culture gap that can impede a startup's ability to attract, retain, and motivate a high-performing team. Prioritizing a positive and inclusive corporate culture is essential for building a resilient and thriving workplace.

Overlooking the Importance of Continuous Learning in Professional Development

Chapter 60: The Learning Void

In the ever-evolving landscape of Innovaria, a team led by Morgan aimed to stay at the forefront of artificial intelligence innovation. Focused on technical expertise, the team inadvertently overlooked the crucial importance of continuous learning in professional development.

As the industry advanced, the learning void became evident. The absence of a culture of continuous learning left team members struggling to keep up with the latest technologies and industry trends. Neglecting professional development not only hindered individual growth but also impacted the startup's ability to innovate and stay competitive.

Impact:

The consequences were evident in outdated skills, difficulties in adapting to new technologies, and challenges in attracting top talent. Competitors with a strong emphasis on continuous learning showcased a more agile and informed approach, leaving Morgan's startup at a disadvantage in the rapidly evolving field of artificial intelligence.

Recognizing the importance of continuous learning, Morgan and the leadership team implemented training programs, encouraged certifications, and fostered a culture of curiosity and exploration. However, the initial oversight had already led to skills gaps and a need for proactive measures to upskill the team.

The lesson learned was clear: in dynamic industries, overlooking the importance of continuous learning creates a learning void that can impede both individual and organizational growth. Prioritizing professional development and fostering a culture of continuous learning is essential for staying competitive and innovative in rapidly evolving fields.

Disregarding the Importance of Transparent Communication in Leadership

Chapter 61: The Communication Chasm

In the dynamic entrepreneurial realm of Innovaria, a team led by Taylor set out to revolutionize project management solutions. Focused on achieving goals, the team inadvertently disregarded the crucial importance of transparent communication in leadership.

As the startup encountered challenges and changes in project directions, the communication chasm became evident. The lack of clear and transparent communication from leadership led to confusion among team members, fostering a sense of uncertainty and hindering collaboration. Neglecting transparent communication not only impacted morale but also hindered the team's ability to navigate complexities effectively.

Impact:

The consequences were evident in decreased team cohesion, increased misunderstandings, and challenges in meeting project deadlines. Competitors with leaders who prioritized transparent communication showcased a more unified and informed team, leaving Taylor's startup struggling to bridge the communication gap.

Recognizing the importance of transparent communication, Taylor and the leadership team implemented regular updates, open forums for discussion, and a commitment to providing clear guidance. However, the initial disregard had already led to a fractured communication landscape that required concerted efforts to rebuild.

The lesson learned was clear: transparent communication is a cornerstone of effective leadership, and disregarding its importance creates a communication chasm that can hinder a startup's ability to thrive. Prioritizing open and clear communication is essential for fostering a collaborative and resilient team.

Underestimating the Impact of Work-Life Balance on Employee Well-being

Chapter 62: The Balance Dilemma

In the fast-paced environment of Innovaria, a team led by Alex ventured into developing cutting-edge virtual reality solutions. Focused on ambitious goals, the team inadvertently underestimated the profound impact of work-life balance on employee well-being.

As the demands of project deadlines intensified, the balance dilemma became evident. Team members faced burnout, increased stress, and a decline in overall well-being. Neglecting the importance of work-life balance not only impacted employee health but also led to decreased productivity and motivation.

Impact:

The consequences were evident in increased absenteeism, higher turnover rates, and challenges in maintaining a positive team culture. Competitors with a focus on work-life balance showcased a more engaged and satisfied workforce, leaving Alex's startup at a disadvantage in talent retention and overall team performance.

Recognizing the importance of work-life balance, Alex and the leadership team implemented flexible work schedules, encouraged time off, and fostered a culture that valued well-being. However, the initial underestimation had already led to challenges in team dynamics and the need for a concerted effort to prioritize work-life balance.

The lesson learned was clear: work-life balance is integral to employee well-being, and underestimating its impact creates a balance dilemma that can impede a startup's ability to attract and retain top talent. Prioritizing work-life balance is not just a perk but a strategic imperative for building a healthy and high-performing team.

Neglecting the Role of Emotional Intelligence in Leadership Effectiveness

Chapter 63: The Emotion Blindness

In the ever-evolving landscape of Innovaria, a team led by Morgan delved into developing innovative solutions in augmented reality. Focused on technical expertise, the team inadvertently neglected the crucial role of emotional intelligence in leadership effectiveness.

As the startup faced challenges and team dynamics evolved, the emotion blindness became evident. Leaders lacked the ability to empathize with team members, address conflicts, and inspire motivation effectively. Neglecting emotional intelligence not only hindered leadership effectiveness but also impacted team morale and collaboration.

Impact:

The consequences were evident in increased tension among team members, challenges in resolving conflicts, and difficulties in maintaining a positive work culture. Competitors with emotionally intelligent leaders showcased more effective communication and collaboration, leaving Morgan's startup struggling to foster a supportive team environment.

Recognizing the importance of emotional intelligence, Morgan and the leadership team underwent training, actively practiced empathy, and prioritized open communication. However, the initial neglect had already led to interpersonal challenges that required dedicated efforts to overcome.

The lesson learned was clear: emotional intelligence is a cornerstone of effective leadership, and neglecting its role creates an emotion blindness that can hinder a startup's ability to build a cohesive and motivated team. Prioritizing emotional intelligence is essential for fostering positive team dynamics and achieving leadership effectiveness.

Underestimating the Significance of User Experience in Product Success

Chapter 64: The Experience Oversight

In the competitive landscape of Innovaria, a team led by Taylor set out to develop a revolutionary mobile application for productivity. Focused on feature-rich development, the team inadvertently underestimated the critical significance of user experience in product success.

As the mobile app launched, the experience oversight became evident. Users struggled with a confusing interface, encountered usability issues, and faced challenges in navigating the application. Neglecting the importance of user experience not only resulted in negative reviews but also hindered the app's adoption and success in the market.

Impact:

The consequences were evident in low user retention, a decline in app downloads, and challenges in gaining a competitive edge. Competitors with a focus on user-centric design showcased more intuitive and user-friendly applications, leaving Taylor's startup at a disadvantage in the competitive app market.

Recognizing the importance of user experience, Taylor and the development team conducted user testing, gathered feedback, and implemented design improvements. However, the initial oversight had already led to setbacks that required extensive efforts to redesign and reposition the app in the market.

The lesson learned was clear: user experience is a crucial factor in product success, and underestimating its significance creates an experience oversight that can impede a startup's ability to attract and retain users. Prioritizing user-centric design is essential for ensuring the success and sustainability of a product in a competitive market.

Ignoring the Impact of Company Values on Organizational Culture

Chapter 65: The Values Void

In the diverse workplace of Innovaria, a team led by Alex ventured into developing innovative solutions in artificial intelligence. Focused on technological advancements, the team inadvertently ignored the profound impact of company values on organizational culture.

As the startup expanded, the values void became evident. The lack of clear and embraced company values led to a fragmented organizational culture, with team members having varying interpretations of the startup's mission and goals. Ignoring the impact of company values not only created cultural misalignment but also hindered collaboration and a sense of shared purpose.

Impact:

The consequences were evident in decreased employee engagement, challenges in building a cohesive team, and difficulties in fostering a positive work environment. Competitors with well-defined and embraced company values showcased a more unified and motivated workforce, leaving Alex's startup struggling to bridge the values void.

Recognizing the importance of company values, Alex and the leadership team engaged employees in defining and embracing core values, aligning them with the company's mission. However, the initial ignorance had already led to cultural challenges that required intentional efforts to establish a shared set of values.

The lesson learned was clear: company values are the foundation of organizational culture, and ignoring their impact creates a values void that can impede a startup's ability to build a cohesive and motivated team. Prioritizing well-defined and embraced company values is essential for shaping a positive and purpose-driven work environment.

Underestimating the Importance of Crisis Preparedness in Business Continuity

Chapter 66: The Preparedness Gap

In the unpredictable landscape of Innovaria, a team led by Taylor aimed to establish a robust e-commerce platform. Focused on growth and expansion, the team inadvertently underestimated the critical importance of crisis preparedness in ensuring business continuity.

As the startup faced unexpected challenges, the preparedness gap became evident. The lack of a comprehensive crisis management plan left the team scrambling to respond effectively, leading to disruptions in operations and customer dissatisfaction. Underestimating the importance of crisis preparedness not only posed risks to the startup's reputation but also hindered its ability to navigate unforeseen circumstances.

Impact:

The consequences were evident in revenue loss, damage to brand reputation, and challenges in rebuilding customer trust. Competitors with robust crisis preparedness plans showcased a more resilient response to challenges, leaving Taylor's startup at a disadvantage in maintaining business continuity.

Recognizing the importance of crisis preparedness, Taylor and the leadership team developed and implemented a comprehensive crisis management plan, including communication strategies and risk mitigation measures. However, the initial underestimation had already led to setbacks that required strategic realignment and dedicated efforts to regain customer confidence.

The lesson learned was clear: crises are inevitable, and underestimating the importance of crisis preparedness creates a preparedness gap that can have far-reaching consequences. Prioritizing proactive crisis planning is essential for safeguarding business continuity and reputation in the face of unforeseen challenges.

Neglecting the Impact of Regulatory Compliance on Business Operations

Chapter 67: The Compliance Oversight

In the regulated landscape of Innovaria, a team led by Morgan ventured into the development of financial technology solutions. Focused on innovation, the team inadvertently neglected the critical impact of regulatory compliance on business operations.

As the startup gained traction, the compliance oversight became evident. The lack of adherence to regulatory requirements led to legal challenges, fines, and disruptions in business operations. Neglecting regulatory compliance not only posed financial risks but also hindered the startup's ability to establish trust with customers and partners.

Impact:

The consequences were evident in legal complications, financial penalties, and challenges in rebuilding a tarnished reputation. Competitors with a strong focus on regulatory compliance showcased a commitment to legal standards, leaving Morgan's startup at a disadvantage in the tightly regulated industry.

Recognizing the importance of regulatory compliance, Morgan and the team implemented robust compliance protocols, engaged legal experts, and conducted regular audits. However, the initial oversight had already led to legal repercussions that required significant resources to address.

The lesson learned was clear: regulatory compliance is non-negotiable, and neglecting its impact creates a compliance oversight that can jeopardize a startup's legal standing and reputation. Prioritizing a proactive approach to regulatory compliance is essential for ensuring the sustainability and trustworthiness of business operations.

Underestimating the Role of Networking in Business Growth

Chapter 68: The Networking Void

In the interconnected business environment of Innovaria, a team led by Taylor aimed to establish a niche in the software development industry. Focused on product excellence, the team inadvertently underestimated the pivotal role of networking in fostering business growth.

As the startup sought market recognition, the networking void became evident. The lack of a robust networking strategy left the team with limited industry connections, hindering opportunities for partnerships, collaborations, and potential business leads. Underestimating the role of networking not only impacted visibility but also limited the startup's ability to tap into valuable resources.

Impact:

The consequences were evident in missed collaborations, challenges in accessing industry insights, and difficulties in securing funding. Competitors with a strong emphasis on networking showcased a more expansive reach and diverse opportunities, leaving Taylor's startup at a disadvantage in the competitive software development landscape.

Recognizing the importance of networking, Taylor and the team actively participated in industry events, joined professional organizations, and cultivated relationships with key stakeholders. However, the initial underestimation had already led to missed opportunities that required proactive networking efforts to overcome.

The lesson learned was clear: in business, who you know matters, and underestimating the role of networking creates a networking void that can impede a startup's growth potential. Prioritizing strategic networking is essential for building valuable connections, fostering collaborations, and unlocking opportunities for business expansion.

Neglecting the Importance of Mental Health Support in the Workplace

Chapter 69: The Mental Health Gap

In the progressive workplace culture of Innovaria, a team led by Alex delved into the development of innovative health and wellness applications. Focused on productivity, the team inadvertently neglected the crucial importance of mental health support in the workplace.

As the demands of projects intensified, the mental health gap became evident. Team members faced increased stress, burnout, and a decline in overall well-being. Neglecting mental health support not only impacted employee health but also led to decreased productivity, higher turnover rates, and challenges in maintaining a positive work culture.

Impact:

The consequences were evident in increased absenteeism, decreased team morale, and difficulties in attracting and retaining top talent. Competitors with a focus on mental health support showcased a more compassionate and supportive work environment, leaving Alex's startup at a disadvantage in talent retention and overall team well-being.

Recognizing the importance of mental health support, Alex and the leadership team implemented employee assistance programs, mental health awareness initiatives, and policies that prioritized work-life balance. However, the initial neglect had already led to cultural challenges that required dedicated efforts to bridge the mental health gap.

The lesson learned was clear: neglecting the importance of mental health support creates a mental health gap that can have profound effects on employee well-being and organizational success. Prioritizing mental health initiatives is essential for fostering a supportive workplace culture and ensuring the overall health and resilience of the team.

Overlooking the Potential of Strategic Partnerships for Business Expansion

Chapter 70: The Partnership Blind Spot

In the collaborative landscape of Innovaria, a team led by Taylor aimed to establish a foothold in the rapidly evolving tech industry. Focused on independent growth, the team inadvertently overlooked the immense potential of strategic partnerships for business expansion.

As the startup faced the challenges of scaling, the partnership blind spot became evident. The lack of a proactive approach to forming strategic alliances left the team with limited access to resources, expertise, and market opportunities. Overlooking the potential of strategic partnerships not only hindered growth but also limited the startup's ability to navigate industry challenges effectively.

Impact:

The consequences were evident in missed business opportunities, challenges in accessing new markets, and difficulties in staying competitive. Competitors with a focus on strategic partnerships showcased a more diversified and resilient approach to business expansion, leaving Taylor's startup at a disadvantage in the dynamic tech landscape.

Recognizing the potential of strategic partnerships, Taylor and the team actively sought collaborations, formed alliances with industry leaders, and leveraged complementary strengths. However, the initial oversight had already led to missed opportunities that required strategic efforts to establish impactful partnerships.

The lesson learned was clear: in the interconnected business world, strategic partnerships can be a catalyst for growth, and overlooking their potential creates a partnership blind spot that can impede a startup's ability to expand effectively. Prioritizing strategic alliances is essential for unlocking new opportunities, accessing valuable resources, and fostering long-term business success.

Underestimating the Importance of Brand Consistency in Marketing

Chapter 71: The Consistency Gap

In the competitive marketing landscape of Innovaria, a team led by Morgan set out to establish a strong presence in the digital marketing space. Focused on creativity, the team inadvertently underestimated the critical importance of brand consistency in marketing.

As the startup deployed various marketing campaigns, the consistency gap became evident. Inconsistent messaging, visual elements, and brand identity led to confusion among the target audience and hindered the establishment of a strong brand presence. Underestimating the importance of brand consistency not only affected brand recognition but also limited the effectiveness of marketing efforts.

Impact:

The consequences were evident in decreased brand trust, challenges in building a loyal customer base, and difficulties in standing out in a crowded market. Competitors with a focus on brand consistency showcased a more cohesive and recognizable brand image, leaving Morgan's startup at a disadvantage in the highly competitive digital marketing landscape.

Recognizing the importance of brand consistency, Morgan and the marketing team implemented brand guidelines, standardized messaging, and visual elements across all channels. However, the initial underestimation had already led to a consistency gap that required concerted efforts to align and strengthen the brand identity.

The lesson learned was clear: brand consistency is a cornerstone of effective marketing, and underestimating its importance creates a consistency gap that can impede a startup's ability to build a strong brand presence. Prioritizing brand consistency is essential for establishing trust, increasing brand recognition, and enhancing the impact of marketing initiatives.

Neglecting the Role of Data Privacy in Customer Trust

Chapter 72: The Privacy Oversight

In the era of data-driven innovation in Innovaria, a team led by Taylor ventured into developing cutting-edge artificial intelligence solutions. Focused on technological advancements, the team inadvertently neglected the crucial role of data privacy in building and maintaining customer trust.

As the startup collected and processed vast amounts of data, the privacy oversight became evident. Insufficient measures to safeguard user information led to concerns about data security and privacy breaches. Neglecting the importance of data privacy not only posed risks to customer trust but also invited legal and regulatory challenges.

Impact:

The consequences were evident in decreased customer confidence, reputational damage, and legal ramifications. Competitors with a strong focus on data privacy showcased a commitment to protecting user information, leaving Taylor's startup at a disadvantage in gaining customer trust.

Recognizing the importance of data privacy, Taylor and the team implemented robust data protection measures, updated privacy policies, and ensured compliance with relevant regulations. However, the initial oversight had already led to reputational challenges that required dedicated efforts to rebuild trust.

The lesson learned was clear: data privacy is a critical component of customer trust, and neglecting its role creates a privacy oversight that can have far-reaching consequences. Prioritizing data protection measures is essential for safeguarding customer trust, maintaining a positive brand image, and mitigating the risks associated with data-driven innovations.

Underestimating the Impact of Employee Recognition on Morale

Chapter 73: The Recognition Gap

In the collaborative workspace of Innovaria, a team led by Alex aimed to revolutionize cloud computing solutions. Focused on technical excellence, the team inadvertently underestimated the profound impact of employee recognition on morale.

As the startup expanded, the recognition gap became evident. The lack of a systematic approach to acknowledging and appreciating employee contributions led to decreased morale and diminished motivation. Underestimating the importance of employee recognition not only affected individual job satisfaction but also hindered overall team performance.

Impact:

The consequences were evident in increased turnover rates, difficulties in attracting top talent, and challenges in maintaining a positive work culture. Competitors with a focus on employee recognition showcased a more engaged and motivated workforce, leaving Alex's startup at a disadvantage in talent retention and team cohesion.

Recognizing the importance of employee recognition, Alex and the leadership team implemented regular acknowledgment programs, celebrated achievements, and fostered a culture of appreciation. However, the initial underestimation had already led to cultural challenges that required dedicated efforts to bridge the recognition gap.

The lesson learned was clear: employee recognition is a powerful driver of morale and performance, and underestimating its impact creates a recognition gap that can impede a startup's ability to retain and motivate a high-performing team. Prioritizing employee recognition is essential for fostering a positive work environment and ensuring the long-term success of the organization.

Neglecting the Importance of Environmental Sustainability in Business Practices

Chapter 74: The Sustainability Blind Spot

In the environmentally conscious landscape of Innovaria, a team led by Taylor set out to develop innovative solutions in renewable energy. Focused on technological advancements, the team inadvertently neglected the crucial importance of environmental sustainability in overall business practices.

As the startup scaled its operations, the sustainability blind spot became evident. Insufficient measures to reduce environmental impact and implement sustainable practices not only contributed to ecological harm but also alienated environmentally conscious customers. Neglecting the importance of environmental sustainability not only posed risks to the planet but also impacted the startup's reputation and market positioning.

IMPACT:

The consequences were evident in decreased customer loyalty, challenges in securing partnerships with sustainable-focused entities, and difficulties in meeting evolving market expectations. Competitors with a strong commitment to environmental sustainability showcased a more responsible approach, leaving Taylor's startup at a disadvantage in the eco-friendly industry.

Recognizing the importance of environmental sustainability, Taylor and the team implemented eco-friendly practices, reduced waste, and adopted renewable energy sources. However, the initial neglect had already led to reputational challenges that required concerted efforts to align with sustainable business practices.

The lesson learned was clear: environmental sustainability is integral to modern business practices, and neglecting its importance creates a sustainability blind spot that can have far-reaching consequences. Prioritizing sustainable practices is essential for meeting market expectations, building a positive brand image, and contributing to a healthier planet.

Underestimating the Impact of Employee Training and Development on Performance

Chapter 75: The Development Void

In the dynamic workplace of Innovaria, a team led by Morgan ventured into developing groundbreaking solutions in the field of biotechnology. Focused on cutting-edge research, the team inadvertently underestimated the profound impact of employee training and development on overall performance.

As the startup faced evolving industry demands, the development void became evident. The lack of a systematic approach to employee training and professional growth led to outdated skills and decreased team effectiveness. Underestimating the importance of continuous learning not only hindered individual career growth but also impacted the startup's ability to innovate and stay competitive.

Underestimating the Impact of Employee Training and Development on Performance

Chapter 75: The Development Void

In the dynamic workplace of Innovaria, a team led by Morgan ventured into developing groundbreaking solutions in the field of biotechnology. Focused on cutting-edge research, the team inadvertently underestimated the profound impact of employee training and development on overall performance.

As the startup faced evolving industry demands, the development void became evident. The lack of a systematic approach to employee training and professional growth led to outdated skills and decreased team effectiveness. Underestimating the importance of continuous learning not only hindered individual career growth but also impacted the startup's ability to innovate and stay competitive.

Impact:

The consequences were evident in decreased productivity, difficulties in adapting to new industry trends, and challenges in attracting top talent. Competitors with a focus on employee training and development showcased a more skilled and adaptable workforce, leaving Morgan's startup at a disadvantage in the rapidly evolving biotechnology landscape.

Recognizing the importance of employee training and development, Morgan and the leadership team implemented continuous learning programs, provided opportunities for skill enhancement, and encouraged professional development. However, the initial underestimation had already led to skills gaps that required strategic efforts to upskill the team.

The lesson learned was clear: employee training and development are vital for individual and organizational success, and underestimating their impact creates a development void that can impede a startup's ability to stay competitive. Prioritizing continuous learning is essential for fostering a skilled and agile workforce, driving innovation, and ensuring long-term success.

Impact:

The consequences were evident in decreased productivity, difficulties in adapting to new industry trends, and challenges in attracting top talent. Competitors with a focus on employee training and development showcased a more skilled and adaptable workforce, leaving Morgan's startup at a disadvantage in the rapidly evolving biotechnology landscape.

Recognizing the importance of employee training and development, Morgan and the leadership team implemented continuous learning programs, provided opportunities for skill enhancement, and encouraged professional development. However, the initial underestimation had already led to skills gaps that required strategic efforts to upskill the team.

The lesson learned was clear: employee training and development are vital for individual and organizational success, and underestimating their impact creates a development void that can impede a startup's ability to stay competitive. Prioritizing continuous learning is essential for fostering a skilled and agile workforce, driving innovation, and ensuring long-term success.

Neglecting the Role of Agile Project Management in Adaptability

Chapter 76: The Adaptability Gap

In the fast-paced world of Innovaria, a team led by Taylor ventured into developing cutting-edge solutions in artificial intelligence. Focused on ambitious project goals, the team inadvertently neglected the crucial role of agile project management in fostering adaptability.

As the startup encountered unforeseen challenges and shifts in project requirements, the adaptability gap became evident. The lack of an agile project management framework led to delays, inefficiencies, and difficulties in responding swiftly to changing market demands. Neglecting the importance of adaptability not only impacted project timelines but also hindered the startup's ability to navigate uncertainties effectively.

Impact:

The consequences were evident in missed deadlines, increased project costs, and challenges in meeting customer expectations. Competitors with a focus on agile project management showcased a more responsive and adaptable approach, leaving Taylor's startup at a disadvantage in the dynamic field of artificial intelligence.

Recognizing the importance of agile project management, Taylor and the team implemented agile methodologies, iterative processes, and regular feedback loops. However, the initial neglect had already led to setbacks that required a concerted effort to foster adaptability in project execution.

The lesson learned was clear: in a rapidly changing business environment, neglecting the role of agile project management creates an adaptability gap that can impede a startup's ability to respond effectively to market dynamics. Prioritizing agile methodologies is essential for fostering adaptability, improving project outcomes, and ensuring long-term success.

Neglecting the Role of Emotional Well-being in Employee Productivity

Chapter 78: The Productivity Paradox

In the progressive workplace of Innovaria, a team led by Morgan delved into developing innovative solutions in robotics. Focused on technical excellence, the team inadvertently neglected the crucial role of emotional well-being in enhancing employee productivity.

As the demands of ambitious projects intensified, the productivity paradox became evident. Team members faced increased stress, burnout, and a decline in emotional well-being. Neglecting the importance of emotional well-being not only impacted individual mental health but also hindered overall team productivity and collaboration.

Impact:

The consequences were evident in decreased creativity, challenges in teamwork, and difficulties in meeting project milestones. Competitors with a focus on employee well-being showcased a more engaged and productive workforce, leaving Morgan's startup at a disadvantage in innovation and efficiency.

Recognizing the importance of emotional well-being, Morgan and the leadership team implemented wellness programs, mental health resources, and initiatives to foster a supportive work environment. However, the initial neglect had already led to challenges in maintaining a positive team culture that required dedicated efforts to address.

The lesson learned was clear: emotional well-being is integral to productivity, and neglecting its role creates a productivity paradox that can impede a startup's ability to achieve optimal performance. Prioritizing employee well-being is essential for fostering a positive workplace culture, enhancing creativity, and ensuring sustained productivity in the face of challenges.

Underestimating the Significance of Market Research in Product Development

Chapter 79: The Research Void

In the ever-evolving landscape of Innovaria, a team led by Taylor set out to develop cutting-edge solutions in the field of biotechnology. Focused on technological advancements, the team inadvertently underestimated the critical significance of market research in product development.

As the startup introduced new products, the research void became evident. Insufficient market research led to products that did not align with customer needs, preferences, and market trends. Underestimating the importance of market research not only resulted in missed opportunities but also impacted the startup's ability to create products that resonated with the target audience.

Impact:

The consequences were evident in low product adoption rates, challenges in gaining market share, and difficulties in establishing a competitive edge. Competitors with a strong emphasis on market research showcased a more informed and strategic approach, leaving Taylor's startup at a disadvantage in the competitive biotechnology sector.

Recognizing the importance of market research, Taylor and the product development team implemented robust market analysis, customer feedback mechanisms, and data-driven decision-making. However, the initial underestimation had already led to setbacks that required strategic efforts to realign product offerings with market demands.

The lesson learned was clear: market research is a cornerstone of successful product development, and underestimating its significance creates a research void that can impede a startup's ability to create products that resonate with customers. Prioritizing comprehensive market research is essential for understanding customer needs, identifying market trends, and ensuring the success of product offerings.

Ignoring the Role of Corporate Social Responsibility in Building Brand Trust

Chapter 80: The Trust Deficit

In the socially conscious landscape of Innovaria, a team led by Alex aimed to develop groundbreaking solutions in sustainable energy. Focused on technological advancements, the team inadvertently ignored the crucial role of corporate social responsibility (CSR) in building brand trust.

As the startup expanded its operations, the trust deficit became evident. The lack of a comprehensive CSR strategy led to perceptions of environmental neglect and social irresponsibility. Ignoring the role of CSR not only impacted brand trust but also hindered the startup's ability to connect with socially conscious consumers.

Impact:

The consequences were evident in decreased customer loyalty, challenges in securing partnerships with socially responsible organizations, and difficulties in differentiating the brand in a crowded market. Competitors with a strong commitment to CSR showcased a more ethical and sustainable approach, leaving Alex's startup at a disadvantage in the socially conscious energy sector.

Recognizing the importance of corporate social responsibility, Alex and the leadership team implemented sustainability initiatives, community engagement programs, and transparent communication about ethical practices. However, the initial ignorance had already led to a trust deficit that required strategic efforts to rebuild credibility.

The lesson learned was clear: corporate social responsibility is not just a trend but a fundamental aspect of brand trust, and ignoring its role creates a trust deficit that can impact a startup's reputation. Prioritizing CSR is essential for building a positive brand image, connecting with socially conscious consumers, and ensuring long-term sustainability in the market.

Overlooking the Importance of Cybersecurity in Protecting Business Assets

Chapter 81: The Security Gap

In the digitally driven landscape of Innovaria, a team led by Morgan aimed to revolutionize cloud security solutions. Focused on innovation, the team inadvertently overlooked the critical importance of cybersecurity in protecting business assets.

As the startup gained prominence, the security gap became evident. Insufficient measures to safeguard sensitive data led to cybersecurity threats, data breaches, and potential risks to business continuity. Overlooking the importance of cybersecurity not only posed risks to sensitive information but also impacted the startup's reputation and client trust.

Impact:

The consequences were evident in financial losses, damage to brand reputation, and challenges in retaining clients. Competitors with a strong focus on cybersecurity showcased a more secure and trustworthy approach, leaving Morgan's startup at a disadvantage in the competitive cybersecurity industry.

Recognizing the importance of cybersecurity, Morgan and the technology team implemented robust security protocols, encryption measures, and regular cybersecurity audits. However, the initial oversight had already led to security breaches that required significant efforts to rectify and rebuild client confidence.

The lesson learned was clear: cybersecurity is a non-negotiable aspect of modern business, and overlooking its importance creates a security gap that can have severe consequences. Prioritizing robust cybersecurity measures is essential for protecting business assets, maintaining client trust, and ensuring the overall security of the organization.

Underestimating the Impact of Technical Debt on Software Development

Chapter 82: The Debt Dilemma

In the dynamic realm of Innovaria, a team led by Taylor set out to develop cutting-edge software solutions. Focused on rapid development, the team inadvertently underestimated the profound impact of technical debt on software development.

As the startup raced to meet tight deadlines, the debt dilemma became evident. Accumulated technical debt, resulting from shortcuts and expedited coding practices, led to a complex and error-prone codebase. Underestimating the importance of addressing technical debt not only impacted the software's stability but also hindered the team's agility in responding to changing requirements.

Impact:

The consequences were evident in increased development time for new features, challenges in debugging, and difficulties in maintaining software scalability. Competitors with a focus on managing technical debt showcased a more efficient and adaptable development process, leaving Taylor's startup at a disadvantage in the competitive software market.

Recognizing the importance of addressing technical debt, Taylor and the development team implemented regular code reviews, refactoring initiatives, and a strategic approach to debt reduction. However, the initial underestimation had already led to challenges that required concerted efforts to streamline the development process.

The lesson learned was clear: technical debt is a reality in software development, and underestimating its impact creates a debt dilemma that can impede a startup's ability to deliver high-quality software efficiently. Prioritizing the management of technical debt is essential for maintaining a robust codebase, ensuring software stability, and sustaining long-term success.

Neglecting Accessibility in User Interface Design

Chapter 83: The Accessibility Gap

In the user-centric landscape of Innovaria, a team led by Alex focused on developing a state-of-the-art mobile application. In their pursuit of cutting-edge design, the team inadvertently neglected the crucial aspect of accessibility in user interface (UI) design.

As the mobile app launched, the accessibility gap became evident. The lack of consideration for users with diverse abilities led to usability challenges for individuals with disabilities. Neglecting accessibility not only resulted in exclusion but also hindered the app's reach and adoption among a broader user base.

Impact:

The consequences were evident in negative user feedback, potential legal issues related to accessibility compliance, and challenges in reaching a diverse audience. Competitors with a focus on accessible design showcased a more inclusive and user-friendly approach, leaving Alex's startup at a disadvantage in the competitive mobile app market.

Recognizing the importance of accessibility, Alex and the design team implemented accessible design principles, conducted usability testing with individuals with diverse abilities, and ensured compliance with accessibility standards. However, the initial neglect had already led to challenges that required dedicated efforts to make the app more inclusive.

The lesson learned was clear: accessibility is a fundamental aspect of user interface design, and neglecting its importance creates an accessibility gap that can impede a startup's ability to provide an inclusive user experience. Prioritizing accessible design is essential for reaching a diverse audience, improving user satisfaction, and ensuring the usability of products across various user abilities.

Disregarding the Importance of A/B Testing in Marketing Campaigns

Chapter 84: The Testing Oversight

In the data-driven marketing landscape of Innovaria, a team led by Morgan sought to establish a strong digital presence for their new product. Focused on creativity, the team inadvertently disregarded the critical importance of A/B testing in marketing campaigns.

As the marketing efforts unfolded, the testing oversight became evident. The lack of A/B testing led to uncertainties about the effectiveness of different campaign elements. Disregarding the importance of A/B testing not only hindered optimization but also limited the team's ability to understand and respond to audience preferences.

Impact:

The consequences were evident in suboptimal conversion rates, challenges in identifying the most effective messaging, and difficulties in allocating marketing budgets efficiently. Competitors with a focus on A/B testing showcased a more data-informed and adaptive approach, leaving Morgan's startup at a disadvantage in the competitive digital marketing space.

Recognizing the importance of A/B testing, Morgan and the marketing team implemented systematic testing procedures, analyzed campaign performance data, and refined strategies based on real-time insights. However, the initial disregard had already led to missed opportunities that required strategic efforts to enhance campaign effectiveness.

The lesson learned was clear: A/B testing is a cornerstone of effective marketing, and disregarding its importance creates a testing oversight that can impede a startup's ability to optimize campaigns for maximum impact. Prioritizing A/B testing is essential for refining strategies, improving conversion rates, and ensuring a data-driven approach to digital marketing.

Overlooking the Impact of Supply Chain Disruptions on Operations

Chapter 85: The Supply Chain Gap

In the interconnected global market of Innovaria, a team led by Taylor aimed to deliver cutting-edge hardware solutions. Focused on innovation, the team inadvertently overlooked the potential impact of supply chain disruptions on operations.

As the startup scaled its hardware production, the supply chain gap became evident. Unforeseen disruptions, such as geopolitical events and material shortages, led to delays in product delivery and increased production costs. Overlooking the potential impact of supply chain disruptions not only posed operational challenges but also affected customer satisfaction and market competitiveness.

Impact:

The consequences were evident in increased lead times, challenges in meeting customer demand, and difficulties in managing production costs. Competitors with a focus on resilient supply chain management showcased a more adaptable and responsive approach, leaving Taylor's startup at a disadvantage in the competitive hardware industry.

Recognizing the importance of supply chain resilience, Taylor and the operations team implemented risk mitigation strategies, diversified suppliers, and monitored geopolitical factors affecting the supply chain. However, the initial oversight had already led to operational challenges that required strategic efforts to enhance supply chain robustness.

The lesson learned was clear: supply chain disruptions are inherent risks in business, and overlooking their potential impact creates a supply chain gap that can impede a startup's ability to maintain operational efficiency. Prioritizing resilient supply chain management is essential for ensuring timely production, managing costs effectively, and enhancing overall business continuity.

Neglecting the Role of User Feedback in Product Iteration

Chapter 86: The Feedback Void

In the customer-centric landscape of Innovaria, a team led by Alex aimed to continuously improve their flagship software product. Focused on innovation, the team inadvertently neglected the crucial role of user feedback in the iterative development process.

As the software evolved, the feedback void became evident. The lack of a systematic approach to collecting and incorporating user feedback led to a disconnect between the product and user expectations. Neglecting the importance of user feedback not only hindered product iteration but also limited the team's ability to address user needs effectively.

Impact:

The consequences were evident in decreased user satisfaction, challenges in identifying product improvement opportunities, and difficulties in retaining a loyal customer base. Competitors with a focus on user feedback showcased a more responsive and user-centered approach, leaving Alex's startup at a disadvantage in the competitive software market.

Recognizing the importance of user feedback, Alex and the product development team implemented feedback collection mechanisms, conducted usability testing, and prioritized user-driven features. However, the initial neglect had already led to missed opportunities that required concerted efforts to establish a feedback loop with users.

The lesson learned was clear: user feedback is invaluable for product iteration, and neglecting its role creates a feedback void that can impede a startup's ability to deliver a product that resonates with users. Prioritizing continuous user feedback is essential for staying aligned with user expectations, improving product functionality, and ensuring long-term customer satisfaction.

Disregarding the Importance of Data Governance in Big Data Analytics

Chapter 87: The Governance Gap

In the era of data-driven insights in Innovaria, a team led by Morgan ventured into harnessing big data for business analytics. Focused on extracting valuable insights, the team inadvertently disregarded the critical importance of data governance in the big data analytics process.

As the volume of data processed increased, the governance gap became evident. Insufficient measures to ensure data quality, security, and compliance led to inaccuracies in analytical results and potential risks to data privacy. Disregarding the importance of data governance not only posed risks to decision-making but also invited regulatory challenges.

Impact:

The consequences were evident in unreliable analytics outcomes, challenges in building trust in data-driven insights, and potential legal repercussions. Competitors with a focus on robust data governance showcased a more reliable and compliant approach, leaving Morgan's startup at a disadvantage in the competitive big data analytics industry.

Recognizing the importance of data governance, Morgan and the data analytics team implemented comprehensive data quality standards, enhanced security protocols, and ensured compliance with data protection regulations. However, the initial disregard had already led to challenges that required strategic efforts to establish a governance framework.

The lesson learned was clear: data governance is essential for trustworthy analytics, and disregarding its importance creates a governance gap that can impede a startup's ability to derive accurate insights from big data. Prioritizing data governance is essential for ensuring data integrity, maintaining compliance, and harnessing the full potential of big data analytics.

Underestimating the Importance of Employee Cross-Training

Chapter 88: The Skill Silo

In the collaborative workplace of Innovaria, a team led by Taylor aimed to revolutionize automation solutions. Focused on specialized skills, the team inadvertently underestimated the importance of employee cross-training.

As the startup expanded, the skill silo became evident. Team members with specialized expertise faced challenges in collaborating across different aspects of projects. Underestimating the importance of cross-training not only hindered collaboration but also limited the team's adaptability to changing project requirements.

Impact:

The consequences were evident in project delays, difficulties in handling workload fluctuations, and challenges in achieving a holistic understanding of the automation ecosystem. Competitors with a focus on cross-training showcased a more versatile and collaborative approach, leaving Taylor's startup at a disadvantage in the dynamic field of automation.

Recognizing the importance of employee cross-training, Taylor and the leadership team implemented a cross-training program, encouraging team members to develop skills outside their primary expertise. However, the initial underestimation had already led to challenges that required concerted efforts to break down skill silos within the team.

The lesson learned was clear: employee cross-training is crucial for building a versatile and collaborative workforce, and underestimating its importance creates a skill silo that can impede a startup's ability to navigate dynamic project requirements. Prioritizing cross-training initiatives is essential for fostering a culture of adaptability and ensuring the team can collectively address diverse challenges.

Overlooking the Role of Storytelling in Brand Communication

Chapter 89: The Narrative Void

In the competitive market of Innovaria, a team led by Alex aimed to establish a strong brand presence for their innovative gadgets. Focused on product features, the team inadvertently overlooked the crucial role of storytelling in brand communication.

As the marketing campaigns unfolded, the narrative void became evident. The lack of compelling storytelling led to a disconnect with the audience, limiting the emotional connection with the brand. Overlooking the role of storytelling not only affected brand recall but also hindered the ability to create a compelling brand narrative.

Impact:

The consequences were evident in decreased brand engagement, challenges in creating a distinctive brand identity, and difficulties in connecting with consumers on an emotional level. Competitors with a focus on storytelling showcased a more memorable and resonant brand communication approach, leaving Alex's startup at a disadvantage in the competitive gadget market.

Recognizing the importance of storytelling, Alex and the marketing team revamped their communication strategy, incorporating compelling narratives into product launches and brand messaging. However, the initial oversight had already led to missed opportunities that required strategic efforts to establish a meaningful brand narrative.

The lesson learned was clear: storytelling is a powerful tool in brand communication, and overlooking its role creates a narrative void that can impede a startup's ability to connect emotionally with its audience. Prioritizing storytelling in brand communication is essential for creating a memorable brand identity and fostering a deeper connection with consumers.

Disregarding the Importance of Customer Retention in Growth Strategies

Chapter 90: The Retention Gap

In the customer-centric landscape of Innovaria, a team led by Morgan set out to establish a strong foothold in the software services sector. Focused on acquiring new customers, the team inadvertently disregarded the critical importance of customer retention in overall growth strategies.

As the customer base expanded, the retention gap became evident. Insufficient efforts to nurture existing customer relationships and provide ongoing value led to higher churn rates. Disregarding the importance of customer retention not only impacted revenue stability but also hindered the startup's ability to build a loyal customer community.

Impact:

The consequences were evident in declining customer lifetime value, challenges in sustaining revenue growth, and difficulties in maintaining a positive brand reputation. Competitors with a focus on customer retention showcased a more stable and loyal customer base, leaving Morgan's startup at a disadvantage in the competitive software services market.

Recognizing the importance of customer retention, Morgan and the customer success team implemented proactive retention strategies, personalized customer experiences, and loyalty programs. However, the initial disregard had already led to challenges that required strategic efforts to bridge the retention gap.

The lesson learned was clear: customer retention is as vital as customer acquisition in growth strategies, and disregarding its importance creates a retention gap that can impede a startup's ability to achieve sustained growth. Prioritizing customer retention initiatives is essential for building long-term customer relationships, maximizing customer lifetime value, and ensuring the overall success of growth strategies.

NEGLECTING THE IMPACT OF CULTURE ON INNOVATION

Chapter 91: The Innovation Culture Void

In the dynamic environment of Innovaria, a team led by Taylor sought to foster innovation in their biotechnology projects. Focused on technical advancements, the team inadvertently neglected the crucial impact of organizational culture on innovation.

As the projects advanced, the innovation culture void became evident. The lack of a culture that encouraged risk-taking, collaboration, and open communication hindered the team's ability to generate groundbreaking ideas. Neglecting the impact of culture on innovation not only stifled creativity but also limited the startup's ability to stay ahead in a rapidly evolving field.

Impact:

The consequences were evident in a lack of breakthrough innovations, challenges in attracting top talent, and difficulties in adapting to industry disruptions. Competitors with a focus on fostering an innovation-friendly culture showcased a more dynamic and adaptable approach, leaving Taylor's startup at a disadvantage in the competitive biotechnology landscape.

Recognizing the importance of culture in innovation, Taylor and the leadership team implemented initiatives to encourage a culture of experimentation, collaboration, and continuous learning. However, the initial neglect had already led to challenges that required concerted efforts to establish a vibrant innovation culture within the organization.

The lesson learned was clear: organizational culture plays a pivotal role in fostering innovation, and neglecting its impact creates an innovation culture void that can impede a startup's ability to stay at the forefront of industry advancements. Prioritizing a culture that encourages creativity and experimentation is essential for driving innovation and ensuring long-term success.

Underestimating the Importance of Crisis Preparedness

Chapter 92: The Crisis Unpreparedness

In the unpredictable landscape of Innovaria, a team led by Alex ventured into the competitive market of smart home devices. Focused on product development and market expansion, the team inadvertently underestimated the importance of crisis preparedness.

As the startup faced unforeseen challenges, the crisis unpreparedness became evident. Insufficient plans and resources for handling crises, such as product recalls or unforeseen market downturns, left the team scrambling to respond effectively. Underestimating the importance of crisis preparedness not only risked financial stability but also impacted the startup's reputation and customer trust.

Impact:

The consequences were evident in financial losses, challenges in rebuilding brand trust, and difficulties in regaining market share. Competitors with a focus on crisis preparedness showcased a more resilient and responsive approach, leaving Alex's startup at a disadvantage in the competitive smart home industry.

Recognizing the importance of crisis preparedness, Alex and the leadership team implemented comprehensive crisis management plans, communication strategies, and regular scenario drills. However, the initial underestimation had already led to challenges that required strategic efforts to rebuild resilience in the face of unforeseen events.

The lesson learned was clear: crises are inevitable in business, and underestimating the importance of crisis preparedness creates a vulnerability that can have severe consequences. Prioritizing comprehensive crisis management strategies is essential for safeguarding financial stability, maintaining brand reputation, and ensuring a resilient response to unexpected challenges.

Overlooking the Role of Emotional Intelligence in Leadership

Chapter 93: The Leadership Blind Spot

In the evolving workplace of Innovaria, a team led by Morgan aimed to excel in the field of artificial intelligence. Focused on technical expertise, the team inadvertently overlooked the crucial role of emotional intelligence in leadership.

As the projects advanced, the leadership blind spot became evident. The lack of emotional intelligence in leadership led to challenges in team communication, motivation, and collaboration. Overlooking the importance of emotional intelligence not only impacted team dynamics but also hindered the startup's ability to foster a positive and inclusive work environment.

Impact:

The consequences were evident in decreased team morale, challenges in retaining top talent, and difficulties in resolving interpersonal conflicts. Competitors with emotionally intelligent leadership showcased a more empathetic and collaborative approach, leaving Morgan's startup at a disadvantage in the competitive artificial intelligence sector.

Recognizing the importance of emotional intelligence, Morgan and the leadership team underwent training programs, implemented mentorship initiatives, and fostered a culture that valued emotional intelligence in leadership. However, the initial oversight had already led to challenges that required concerted efforts to enhance leadership dynamics within the organization.

The lesson learned was clear: emotional intelligence is integral to effective leadership, and overlooking its role creates a leadership blind spot that can impede a startup's ability to build a cohesive and motivated team. Prioritizing emotional intelligence in leadership is essential for creating a positive work environment, improving team dynamics, and ensuring long-term success.

Neglecting the Importance of Regulatory Compliance in Product Development

Chapter 94: The Compliance Gap

In the regulated landscape of Innovaria, a team led by Taylor aimed to develop advanced medical devices. Focused on technological innovations, the team inadvertently neglected the crucial importance of regulatory compliance in product development.

As the startup advanced its medical devices through development stages, the compliance gap became evident. Insufficient attention to regulatory requirements led to delays in product approvals and potential legal repercussions. Neglecting the importance of regulatory compliance not only impacted time-to-market but also posed risks to the startup's reputation and market credibility.

Impact:

The consequences were evident in missed market opportunities, challenges in gaining regulatory approvals, and difficulties in building trust with healthcare professionals. Competitors with a strong focus on regulatory compliance showcased a more responsible and market-ready approach, leaving Taylor's startup at a disadvantage in the competitive medical device industry.

Recognizing the importance of regulatory compliance, Taylor and the product development team implemented robust compliance processes, engaged regulatory experts early in the development process, and ensured adherence to industry standards. However, the initial neglect had already led to challenges that required strategic efforts to bridge the compliance gap.

The lesson learned was clear: regulatory compliance is non-negotiable in industries with stringent requirements, and neglecting its importance creates a compliance gap that can impede a startup's ability to bring innovative products to market. Prioritizing regulatory compliance is essential for ensuring timely approvals, building market credibility, and navigating regulatory landscapes effectively.

DISREGARDING ENVIRONMENTAL SUSTAINABILITY IN MANUFACTURING PROCESSES

Chapter 95: The Sustainability Oversight

In the environmentally conscious landscape of Innovaria, a team led by Alex aimed to manufacture cutting-edge consumer electronics. Focused on technological advancements, the team inadvertently disregarded the critical importance of environmental sustainability in manufacturing processes.

As the startup scaled its production, the sustainability oversight became evident. Insufficient measures to reduce environmental impact led to increased waste, energy consumption, and carbon footprint. Disregarding the importance of environmental sustainability not only posed risks to the planet but also affected the startup's reputation and consumer trust.

Underestimating the Impact of Geopolitical Factors on Business Operations

Chapter 96: The Geopolitical Blind Spot

In the interconnected global market of Innovaria, a team led by Morgan sought to expand the reach of their artificial intelligence solutions. Focused on technological advancements, the team inadvertently underestimated the impact of geopolitical factors on business operations.

As the startup expanded internationally, the geopolitical blind spot became evident. Unforeseen political developments, trade tensions, and regulatory changes had direct implications on the startup's operations. Underestimating the importance of understanding and navigating geopolitical factors not only posed risks to international expansion but also impacted market competitiveness.

Impact:

The consequences were evident in negative public perception, challenges in meeting sustainability regulations, and difficulties in attracting environmentally conscious consumers. Competitors with a focus on sustainable manufacturing showcased a more responsible and eco-friendly approach, leaving Alex's startup at a disadvantage in the competitive consumer electronics market.

Recognizing the importance of environmental sustainability, Alex and the operations team implemented eco-friendly manufacturing practices, engaged in recycling initiatives, and communicated transparently about sustainability efforts. However, the initial oversight had already led to challenges that required strategic efforts to establish a more sustainable manufacturing approach.

The lesson learned was clear: environmental sustainability is integral to responsible business practices, and disregarding its importance creates a sustainability oversight that can impede a startup's ability to meet evolving consumer expectations. Prioritizing sustainable manufacturing is essential for reducing environmental impact, enhancing brand reputation, and aligning with global sustainability goals.

Overlooking Diversity and Inclusion in Team Building

Chapter 97: The Diversity Gap

In the inclusive workplace of Innovaria, a team led by Taylor aimed to excel in developing cutting-edge robotics solutions. Focused on technical expertise, the team inadvertently overlooked the crucial importance of diversity and inclusion in team building.

As the startup expanded its workforce, the diversity gap became evident. Insufficient efforts to build a diverse and inclusive team led to a lack of varied perspectives and hindered creativity. Overlooking the importance of diversity and inclusion not only impacted team dynamics but also limited the startup's ability to innovate and adapt to diverse market needs.

Impact:

The consequences were evident in decreased innovation, challenges in attracting top talent, and difficulties in understanding and catering to diverse customer needs. Competitors with a focus on diversity and inclusion showcased a more dynamic and adaptable approach, leaving Taylor's startup at a disadvantage in the competitive robotics industry.

Recognizing the importance of diversity and inclusion, Taylor and the HR team implemented initiatives to promote diversity in hiring, foster an inclusive workplace culture, and provide equal opportunities for professional growth. However, the initial oversight had already led to challenges that required strategic efforts to bridge the diversity gap within the organization.

The lesson learned was clear: diversity and inclusion are essential for fostering innovation and adaptability, and overlooking their importance creates a diversity gap that can impede a startup's ability to thrive in a dynamic and globalized market. Prioritizing diversity and inclusion in team building is essential for tapping into varied perspectives, improving creativity, and ensuring long-term success.

Disregarding the Importance of Mental Health Support in the Workplace

Chapter 98: The Mental Health Void

In the progressive workplace of Innovaria, a team led by Alex aimed to create a culture of innovation and productivity. Focused on achieving ambitious goals, the team inadvertently disregarded the critical importance of mental health support in the workplace.

As the startup faced high-pressure situations, the mental health void became evident. Insufficient resources and attention to mental health support led to increased stress, burnout, and decreased employee well-being. Disregarding the importance of mental health not only impacted individual performance but also posed risks to team morale and overall organizational productivity.

Impact:

The consequences were evident in increased absenteeism, challenges in retaining top talent, and difficulties in fostering a positive workplace culture. Competitors with a focus on mental health support showcased a more compassionate and employee-centric approach, leaving Alex's startup at a disadvantage in the competitive innovation landscape.

Recognizing the importance of mental health, Alex and the leadership team implemented mental health programs, provided resources for stress management, and fostered an open dialogue about mental well-being. However, the initial disregard had already led to challenges that required concerted efforts to establish a supportive mental health environment within the organization.

The lesson learned was clear: mental health support is integral to employee well-being and organizational success, and disregarding its importance creates a mental health void that can impede a startup's ability to cultivate a thriving and productive workplace. Prioritizing mental health initiatives is essential for promoting a positive work environment, improving employee retention, and ensuring the holistic well-being of the workforce.

Ignoring the Impact of Emerging Technologies on Market Disruption

Chapter 99: The Disruption Blindness

In the rapidly evolving landscape of Innovaria, a team led by Morgan sought to establish a dominant position in the field of augmented reality. Focused on current technologies, the team inadvertently ignored the profound impact of emerging technologies on market disruption.

As the startup advanced its augmented reality solutions, the disruption blindness became evident. Insufficient attention to emerging technologies, such as mixed reality and spatial computing, left the team vulnerable to being overtaken by more innovative competitors. Ignoring the impact of emerging technologies not only posed risks to market relevance but also hindered the startup's ability to lead in a dynamic tech industry.

Impact:

The consequences were evident in decreased market share, challenges in adapting to evolving customer expectations, and difficulties in staying ahead of industry trends. Competitors with a focus on emerging technologies showcased a more forward-thinking and adaptive approach, leaving Morgan's startup at a disadvantage in the competitive augmented reality sector.

Recognizing the importance of staying abreast of emerging technologies, Morgan and the technology team implemented ongoing technology scouting, research and development initiatives, and partnerships with innovators in the field. However, the initial ignorance had already led to challenges that required strategic efforts to overcome the disruption blindness.

The lesson learned was clear: emerging technologies drive market disruption, and ignoring their impact creates a disruption blindness that can impede a startup's ability to lead in a rapidly changing industry. Prioritizing continuous innovation and staying informed about emerging technologies is essential for staying ahead of the competition and ensuring sustained market relevance.

Failing to Learn from Mistakes

Chapter 100: The Learning Curve

In the concluding chapter of our startup journey, the overarching mistake that looms is the failure to learn from mistakes. Across Innovaria, from Taylor's automation solutions to Alex's consumer electronics and Morgan's artificial intelligence endeavors, each team encountered challenges, missteps, and unforeseen obstacles. Yet, the most significant mistake was the failure to extract valuable lessons from these experiences.

As the startup landscape evolved, the learning curve became a crucial factor in determining success. Failing to learn from mistakes not only perpetuated the repetition of errors but also hindered the teams' ability to adapt, innovate, and thrive in a dynamic environment.

Impact:

The consequences were evident in a lack of organizational growth, challenges in building a resilient and adaptive culture, and difficulties in sustaining long-term success. Competitors with a focus on continuous improvement showcased a more agile and learning-oriented approach, leaving the stagnant startups at a disadvantage in the ever-changing business landscape.

Recognizing the importance of learning from mistakes, the leaders—Taylor, Alex, and Morgan—implemented a culture of continuous improvement, regular post-mortems after projects, and knowledge-sharing initiatives across teams. However, the initial failure to learn had already led to missed opportunities and setbacks that required intentional efforts to break through the stagnation.

The lesson learned was clear: the ability to learn from mistakes is fundamental to a startup's resilience and growth, and failing to prioritize this learning curve can impede progress. Prioritizing a culture of continuous improvement, embracing failure as a learning opportunity, and institutionalizing knowledge-sharing mechanisms are essential for navigating the uncertainties of the startup journey.

Neglecting Financial Forecasting and Planning

Chapter 101: The Forecast Oversight

In the financially driven world of Innovaria, a team led by Taylor aimed to revolutionize financial technology. Focused on cutting-edge solutions, the team inadvertently neglected the crucial importance of financial forecasting and planning.

As the startup expanded its financial services, the forecast oversight became evident. Insufficient attention to accurate financial projections led to budget overruns, inadequate cash flow management, and challenges in securing additional funding. Neglecting the importance of financial forecasting not only impacted financial stability but also hindered the startup's ability to make informed strategic decisions.

Impact:

The consequences were evident in missed growth opportunities, challenges in meeting financial obligations, and difficulties in securing investor confidence. Competitors with a focus on robust financial forecasting showcased a more financially prudent and strategic approach, leaving Taylor's startup at a disadvantage in the competitive financial technology sector.

Recognizing the importance of financial forecasting, Taylor and the finance team implemented comprehensive financial modeling, scenario planning, and regular budget reviews. However, the initial oversight had already led to financial challenges that required strategic efforts to establish a more financially resilient foundation.

The lesson learned was clear: accurate financial forecasting is essential for strategic decision-making, and neglecting its importance creates a forecast oversight that can impede a startup's financial stability. Prioritizing meticulous financial planning is crucial for managing cash flow, securing funding, and ensuring the overall financial health of the startup.

Overlooking the Impact of Currency Fluctuations on International Operations

Chapter 102: The Forex Blind Spot

In the globally connected marketplace of Innovaria, a team led by Alex sought to expand their e-commerce platform internationally. Focused on market access, the team inadvertently overlooked the impact of currency fluctuations on international operations.

As the startup conducted cross-border transactions, the forex blind spot became evident. Unforeseen currency fluctuations led to increased costs, pricing challenges, and potential revenue losses. Overlooking the importance of currency risk management not only impacted financial performance but also posed risks to the startup's international expansion strategy.

Impact:

The consequences were evident in decreased profit margins, challenges in pricing products competitively, and difficulties in predicting financial outcomes. Competitors with a focus on forex risk management showcased a more adaptive and financially strategic approach, leaving Alex's startup at a disadvantage in the competitive e-commerce landscape.

Recognizing the importance of currency risk management, Alex and the finance team implemented hedging strategies, closely monitored exchange rate trends, and revised pricing structures to account for currency fluctuations. However, the initial oversight had already led to financial challenges that required strategic efforts to establish a more resilient financial strategy for international operations.

The lesson learned was clear: currency fluctuations can significantly impact financial performance, and overlooking their importance creates a forex blind spot that can impede a startup's ability to navigate international markets successfully. Prioritizing effective forex risk management is crucial for ensuring financial stability and optimizing international expansion strategies.

Underestimating the Impact of Economic Downturns on Revenue Streams

Chapter 103: The Recession Blindness

In the ever-changing economic landscape of Innovaria, a team led by Morgan aimed to provide innovative consulting services. Focused on market demand, the team inadvertently underestimated the impact of economic downturns on revenue streams.

As the startup scaled its consulting services, the recession blindness became evident. The team's reliance on consistent market demand left them vulnerable to economic downturns, leading to decreased client budgets and project cancellations. Underestimating the importance of economic resilience not only impacted revenue streams but also posed risks to the startup's financial sustainability.

Impact:

The consequences were evident in declining revenues, challenges in maintaining client relationships, and difficulties in adapting to changing economic conditions. Competitors with a focus on economic resilience showcased a more adaptive and financially strategic approach, leaving Morgan's startup at a disadvantage in the competitive consulting industry.

Recognizing the importance of economic resilience, Morgan and the business development team implemented diversified revenue streams, client retention strategies, and contingency plans for economic uncertainties. However, the initial underestimation had already led to financial challenges that required strategic efforts to establish a more resilient financial model.

The lesson learned was clear: economic downturns are inherent risks in business, and underestimating their impact creates a recession blindness that can impede a startup's ability to weather financial challenges. Prioritizing economic resilience is essential for diversifying revenue streams, maintaining financial sustainability, and ensuring long-term success.

Ignoring the Importance of Cost Control in Scaling Operations

Chapter 104: The Cost Expansion Trap

In the ambitious scaling efforts of Innovaria, a team led by Taylor endeavored to expand its cloud computing services. Focused on capturing market share, the team inadvertently ignored the crucial importance of cost control in scaling operations.

As the startup scaled its infrastructure and services, the cost expansion trap became evident. Insufficient attention to controlling operational costs led to increased expenses, decreased profit margins, and challenges in achieving profitability despite revenue growth. Ignoring the importance of cost control not only impacted financial performance but also posed risks to the startup's long-term sustainability.

Impact:

The consequences were evident in declining profitability, challenges in achieving cost-efficiency, and difficulties in sustaining competitive pricing. Competitors with a focus on meticulous cost control showcased a more financially prudent and sustainable approach, leaving Taylor's startup at a disadvantage in the competitive cloud computing sector.

Recognizing the importance of cost control, Taylor and the finance team implemented rigorous cost monitoring, efficiency measures, and regular cost audits. However, the initial oversight had already led to financial challenges that required strategic efforts to establish a more sustainable financial model for scaling operations.

The lesson learned was clear: scaling operations without meticulous cost control can lead to the cost expansion trap, impeding a startup's ability to achieve profitability and financial sustainability. Prioritizing effective cost control measures is crucial for ensuring operational efficiency, maximizing profitability, and building a financially resilient foundation for scaling efforts.

Neglecting Cybersecurity in Financial Technology Solutions

Chapter 105: The Security Oversight

In the dynamic world of financial technology at Innovaria, a team led by Alex aimed to provide secure and innovative payment solutions. Focused on technological advancements, the team inadvertently neglected the crucial importance of cybersecurity in financial technology solutions.

As the startup introduced its payment platforms, the security oversight became evident. Insufficient measures to ensure robust cybersecurity led to data breaches, financial losses, and challenges in gaining trust from users and partners. Neglecting the importance of cybersecurity not only impacted the startup's reputation but also posed risks to the financial well-being of users.

Impact:

The consequences were evident in loss of customer trust, challenges in regulatory compliance, and difficulties in recovering from financial and reputational damage. Competitors with a focus on cybersecurity showcased a more secure and trust-worthy approach, leaving Alex's startup at a disadvantage in the competitive financial technology sector.

Recognizing the importance of cybersecurity, Alex and the technology team implemented stringent security protocols, regular security audits, and compliance with industry standards. However, the initial oversight had already led to challenges that required strategic efforts to establish a more secure and resilient cybersecurity framework.

The lesson learned was clear: cybersecurity is integral to the success of financial technology solutions, and neglecting its importance creates a security oversight that can impede a startup's ability to gain trust and thrive in a competitive market. Prioritizing robust cybersecurity measures is essential for safeguarding user data, maintaining regulatory compliance, and ensuring the long-term success of financial technology solutions.

Overlooking the Impact of Interest Rates on Financing Strategies

Chapter 106: The Interest Rate Blind Spot

In the financially intricate landscape of Innovaria, a team led by Morgan sought to expand its real estate ventures. Focused on strategic acquisitions, the team inadvertently overlooked the impact of interest rates on financing strategies.

As the startup pursued real estate investments, the interest rate blind spot became evident. Unforeseen changes in interest rates led to increased financing costs, challenges in managing debt, and potential impacts on project profitability. Overlooking the importance of interest rate risk management not only impacted financial performance but also posed risks to the startup's ability to execute its real estate strategy.

IMPACT:

The consequences were evident in decreased project profitability, challenges in securing favorable financing, and difficulties in adapting to changing economic conditions. Competitors with a focus on interest rate risk management showcased a more financially strategic approach, leaving Morgan's startup at a disadvantage in the competitive real estate market.

Recognizing the importance of interest rate risk, Morgan and the finance team implemented strategies such as fixed-rate financing, interest rate hedging, and scenario planning for interest rate fluctuations. However, the initial blind spot had already led to financial challenges that required strategic efforts to establish a more resilient financing strategy.

The lesson learned was clear: interest rates play a crucial role in financing strategies, and overlooking their impact creates an interest rate blind spot that can impede a startup's ability to navigate complex financial landscapes. Prioritizing interest rate risk management is essential for optimizing financing structures, ensuring financial stability, and enhancing the overall resilience of the startup.

Neglecting the Importance of Regulatory Compliance in FinTech Innovation

Chapter 107: The Compliance Gap in FinTech

In the highly regulated domain of Innovaria's financial technology ventures, a team led by Taylor aspired to introduce groundbreaking blockchain solutions. Focused on technological innovation, the team inadvertently neglected the crucial importance of regulatory compliance in FinTech.

As the startup rolled out its blockchain products, the compliance gap became evident. Insufficient attention to regulatory requirements led to legal challenges, fines, and potential disruptions to the innovative projects. Neglecting the importance of regulatory compliance not only impacted the startup's legal standing but also posed risks to the broader adoption of its cutting-edge financial technologies.

Impact:

The consequences were evident in legal battles, challenges in obtaining necessary licenses, and difficulties in gaining trust from financial institutions. Competitors with a focus on regulatory compliance showcased a more responsible and legally secure approach, leaving Taylor's startup at a disadvantage in the competitive FinTech landscape.

Recognizing the importance of regulatory compliance, Taylor and the legal team implemented comprehensive compliance checks, engaged regulatory experts early in the development process, and ensured adherence to financial regulations. However, the initial oversight had already led to legal challenges that required strategic efforts to bridge the compliance gap.

The lesson learned was clear: regulatory compliance is non-negotiable in the FinTech industry, and neglecting its importance creates a compliance gap that can impede a startup's ability to innovate within legal boundaries. Prioritizing regulatory compliance is essential for navigating legal landscapes, ensuring the legality of financial products, and building trust with regulators and stakeholders.

Underestimating the Impact of Economic Policies on Investment Strategies

Chapter 108: The Policy Blind Spot

In the intricate world of financial investments at Innovaria, a team led by Alex aimed to excel in wealth management solutions. Focused on maximizing returns, the team inadvertently underestimated the impact of economic policies on investment strategies.

As the startup managed investment portfolios, the policy blind spot became evident. Unforeseen changes in economic policies led to increased market volatility, challenges in predicting market movements, and potential impacts on the performance of investment portfolios. Underestimating the importance of considering economic policy shifts not only impacted financial returns but also posed risks to the startup's reputation as a reliable wealth management partner.

Impact:

The consequences were evident in decreased investment returns, challenges in client retention, and difficulties in adapting to changing economic conditions. Competitors with a focus on economic policy analysis showcased a more adaptive and informed approach, leaving Alex's startup at a disadvantage in the competitive wealth management sector.

Recognizing the importance of economic policy awareness, Alex and the investment team implemented strategies to closely monitor policy changes, conduct regular economic analyses, and adjust investment portfolios based on economic indicators. However, the initial blind spot had already led to financial challenges that required strategic efforts to establish a more resilient investment strategy.

The lesson learned was clear: economic policies significantly impact investment strategies, and underestimating their influence creates a policy blind spot that can impede a startup's ability to navigate financial markets successfully. Prioritizing economic policy analysis is essential for making informed investment decisions, optimizing portfolio performance, and ensuring long-term success in the wealth management industry.

Embracing the Entrepreneurial Odyssey

In the closing chapter of our entrepreneurial odyssey, we reflect on the remarkable journey through the challenges, triumphs, and invaluable lessons encountered by the innovators—Taylor, Alex, and Morgan—in the dynamic landscape of Innovaria. From the inception of cutting-edge technologies to the intricate world of finance, their stories have woven a tapestry of resilience, adaptability, and continuous learning.

As we turn the final pages of "108+ Mistakes That a Startup Makes," it is essential to recognize that each mistake illuminated a path to growth, every setback was an opportunity for resilience, and every lesson learned became a stepping stone toward success. The entrepreneurial journey, with its twists and turns, demands not only courage and determination but also the willingness to embrace failure as a companion on the road to innovation.

In the face of challenges, Taylor, Alex, and Morgan demonstrated the resilience to pivot, the humility to learn, and the courage to persevere.

Their stories serve as beacons for aspiring entrepreneurs navigating the unpredictable terrain of startups. Through technological advancements, financial intricacies, and unforeseen obstacles, they embody the spirit of those who dare to dream, create, and redefine the boundaries of what is possible.

To the entrepreneurs who embark on their own ventures, remember that mistakes are not roadblocks; they are the signposts guiding you toward refinement and growth. With every setback, there is an opportunity to pivot, innovate, and emerge stronger than before. The entrepreneurial journey is a tapestry of experiences, and within its threads lie the lessons that shape the future.

As you forge ahead into the realm of possibilities, may you find inspiration in the stories of those who dared to innovate, learn from the mistakes made in the pursuit of excellence, and celebrate the resilience that defines the entrepreneurial spirit. The road ahead is filled with challenges, but it is also illuminated by the endless possibilities that arise when passion meets perseverance.

Here's to the entrepreneurs who dare to dream, who embrace the journey with open hearts and open minds, and who, in the face of mistakes, setbacks, and challenges, find the courage to redefine success. The entrepreneurial odyssey is an ever-unfolding story—one that invites you to be the author of your own narrative.

As the final chapter concludes, let it be not an end but a new beginning—an invitation to continue the narrative of innovation, growth, and the relentless pursuit of greatness. The journey is yours to chart, the mistakes are yours to learn from, and the triumphs are yours to savor.

Onward, entrepreneur, to new horizons, boundless possibilities, and a future shaped by your vision, tenacity, and unwavering spirit.

The entrepreneurial odyssey continues. May it be filled with inspiration, discovery, and the realization of your most audacious dreams.